BURNING SAGE

BURNING SAGE:

Collected Writings on Unconventional Motherhood, Unconventional Teacherhood, and Unconditional Love

By Jennifer L. Rieger

MINERVA RISING PRESS

Boca Raton

ISBN: 978-1-950811-13-7

Cover Photos
Smoke: Pascal Meier
Sage: Khanh Nguyen
Book design by Brooke Schultz

Printed and bound in USA
First Printing March 2022

Published by Minerva Rising Press
17717 Circle Pond Ct
Boca Raton, FL 33496
www.minervarising.com

For Evan, and all my kids—
past, present, and future

contents

Author's Note:
With the exception of the names noted, I have maintained the
real identities of the people mentioned in these pages. Many
thanks for their permission, love, and support.

Cur moriatur homo, cui salvia cresit in horto?
Why should a man die, whilst Sage grows
in his garden?
— Hildegard of Bingen

This place could be beautiful,
right? You could make this place beautiful.
— Maggie Smith

Plant

The scientific name for sage, Salvia, derives from the Latin word 'salveo' which means 'salvation,' 'to be in good health,' 'to save,' 'to heal.'

ROOTS

Hiding, peeking through the dirt, waiting to trip me up with each casual hit of my Keds. They spread, bubble, unearth, and cling to avoid excavation. It's the avoidance, their obscure nature, that makes me want to dig all the more. With everything.

My dad looks like his mother, and I resemble them both—as if their faces merged into a strange photo app. "The Burnheimers," my dad's family would say. "You look exactly like the Burnheimers." I loved that there was something telling about me—a shadow of the past peeking through, unearthing in a way only time allows. Secrets hidden deep in DNA memory, exposed. But I have yet to find my eyes.

Running through my grandparents' woods, the smell of fresh earth after a rain, my only compass, the sound of their caged beagle howling, guiding me back. The day's harvest nestled securely in the makeshift apron of my shirt—mint, blackberries, sage.

My cousin, Lisa, lives in that house now. The cage is gone, many of those trees, gone; but the house still smells like my grandma, and my footprints linger on the land.

Sprout

A perennial plant, sage grows in spikes with tubular corollas. It attracts bees, butterflies, and hummingbirds.

THE CRUST

My parents grew up in this sleepy little mountain town of Cresson, Pennsylvania, seventy-five miles east of Pittsburgh. Although they moved away shortly after my dad returned home from Vietnam, it was still my childhood home—an escape from the various suburban landscapes of my formative years. It was really a step back in time to a land of walking to James' Drugstore for ice cream and catching fireflies at night with my summer friends. No air conditioning, no locked doors, and a lot of creamy casseroles. Each June, I knew how hard it would be to pedal my mother's old, rusty Schwinn up the steep streets, but by August, my strengthened legs wouldn't even notice the exertion. I spent days studying the cracks in the sidewalk outside of my grandparents' house, knew exactly how many steps it took to get from their backdoor to my great-grandmother's backdoor across the alley, investigated every secret place of that town, memorized the names on cemetery headstones, and lost myself whispering back to the leaves of the nearby woods.

My grandmother became my mother each summer. I believe that she took those nine weeks as a redo for her own naïve parenting. Grandma was an expert in many things—Scrabble, sewing, wallpapering, gardening, folding a perfectly fitted sheet. But my favorite of her talents was baking pies. The red vinyl stool provided the perfect vantage point in Grandma's tiny kitchen. I'd perch all day watching, squirming, questioning as she performed her craft with her gnarled, arthritic hands. The Ecotrin and Darvocet on the windowsill served as constant reminders of her good days and bad, the dull pain and the sharp.

We lived for the good Ecotrin days.

Grandma was an expert multi-tasker who could wield a spoon and rolling pin just as masterfully as a backhanded compliment. If my mother and sister weren't so damaged by the years of dichotomous torment, it could have been comical. Grandma pecked at them—made them question, look in the mirror, say no to the extra donut. My skin was a little thicker; I could take it and dish it. And she respected me. I'd study her as one studies any artist—a dash here, a pinch there, just the right amount of freezing cold water, just the right amount of passive-aggressive sass.

She could be mean to my mother. Really mean. She could also really love her. It didn't take long for me to learn that Grandma had an intense fear of my father's side of the family. He was one of seven, and most of his siblings, nieces, and nephews stayed in Cresson or nearby. With the reality of prospective playmates, Grandma's unfounded anxiety over losing us grew. That fear came out as anger too—sometimes towards my mom, sometimes towards my dad, and even sometimes towards his sisters. I look back on this now and think of all that I missed. Maybe I would have had more time with my cousin, Paige, who eventually became my favorite. Maybe I would be closer to my Aunt Diana, the cool, young aunt whose graduation picture I'd stare at, secretly wishing that one day I would look just like her.[1] Maybe I would have finally been included in the reenactment of *Charlie's Angels* with my sister Kim and my cousins, Shana and Sonya. Maybe they'd finally allow me to be a fourth Angel, instead of Bosley. But Grandma wasn't having it. With each whine of boredom, she'd suggest I play with the children on her street, or find me an entertaining pastime, like pie baking.

It was an art, really. There was never a recipe book or card in sight, never a second-guessing phone call to Texas for reassurance from her own mother. It was an innate skill that was the envy of every pie contest participant at the Cresson's United Methodist Church. The gold-flecked Formica countertop was her palette and the hands crippled by decades of rheumatism and angst were her instruments. They rarely slowed her down. She scooped flour, estimated sugar, nipped at salt and folded butter without a wince or a pause in conversation. *Here, Babydoll. Tear off a piece of that*

---

1 Today, on the rare occasion that I visit Cresson, some stranger invariably tells me that I look like Diana. Genetic goals achieved.

*wax paper for Grandma. Fetch me that pie dish—the deep one.
Make some room in the fridge, darlin'.* I gladly obeyed.

Piecrusts were her specialty. Nobody could mimic, and
nobody tried. The pies were "Grandma's thing." Well, you
girls just don't have patience. You feel the need to handle
the dough too much. I watched, glued to my stool, as she
added ingredients to the separate Pyrex olive-green mixing
bowls. With an old, tin cup that at one time possessed clear
measurements, she combined dry ingredients, blending the
wondrous, silky powder. She set the big bowl aside while
separately preparing her egg, vinegar, and ice water. How a
liquid smelling like my granddad's feet could be turned into
something so heavenly was one of the great mysteries of
the universe. *That's just because you don't understand science yet.
I told you to keep reading those encyclopedias. You'll get it.*

Grating the frozen butter required speed and precision.
If the butter didn't stay cold enough, the crust would be
a failure. Grandma purchased her butter in pound blocks
for this very reason. The quarter sticks were too small and
couldn't "hold the cold." I had once made the mistake of
swiping a few gratings when I thought Grandma wasn't
looking. I loved eating butter, plain. A little obsession that I
eventually grew out of, but nonetheless, I just couldn't help
myself. I put the frozen shavings into my mouth only to spit
them out just as quickly. *Tastes a little like cold Vaseline, hmm?
That's what you get for eating unsalted butter. Lesson learned?* She
didn't miss a trick.

Once the dry, wet, and frozen ingredients were
prepared separately, it was time to fold. Folding was a two-
step process. First, ingredients were coarsely mixed with

a handheld pastry blender, and then Grandma kneaded the dough with her own contorted hands, but only for ten seconds. Apparently, ten seconds is long enough to get everything you're feeling into the dough, without making it too warm. I watched her eyes close and watched her mouth count, without sound. I didn't understand it, but told myself that I still wasn't a scientist and therefore, not a cook, so how could I understand the magic of a kitchen? There was something rhythmic and graceful to the folding, even more so than the final rolling. Grandma's face became stern, like she was teaching that dough a lesson. We knew the face well, and it was not a face easily warmed. Her hands moved beautifully through the dough, and she would stop as abruptly as she started, coming back to her place in this life, this family, this kitchen, this monotony. *There now. That should do it.* Thirty minutes in the refrigerator and then ready for the rolling.

Grandma wiped her hands on the tea towel, poured strawberry Faygo colas, and then directed her attention to us. More often than not, knowing the possibilities of the culinary intermission, my sister would find something else to occupy her time, but my mother stayed put, trying her best to be as cheerful and positive as possible. When it worked, I sipped slowly at the Faygo, letting its sweet fizz capture the moment of peace. When it didn't, I would chug, inevitably resulting in a Faygo reemergence. Sometimes Grandma would inquire about my mother's newly gained five pounds; other times she would rage about how we didn't visit enough. Whatever the complaint, my mother would take it. *You're right, Mother. I think I just need to try harder.* Comments like these would please her, and allow her to lecture on, even if a little more mildly. But there were other times, other piecrusts—crusts that elicited tears.

The sound of the egg timer quickly brought us back to the parallel universe of restrained gluttony, and Grandma retrieved the dough. I hopped from my stool, grabbed the rolling pin, flour, and wax paper for her, and then quickly hopped back out of her way. Her hands carefully balanced the bowl, and then the singing commenced.

"Crazy. I'm crazy for feeling so lonely. I'm crazy. Crazy for feeling so blue…"

She floured, she flattened, she rolled. It was beautiful, comforting, and I had never loved my grandmother more. Every once in awhile I'd join in the soothing Patsy Cline lyrics, and Grandma would smile at the crust; but I knew the smile was for me. Carefully, she lifted the perfect, flattened crust, and placed it on the pie dish, taking her time to press it without getting it too warm. She then scalloped the edge effortlessly, and to this day, I know it was those pained fingers that made the most wondrous ripples of delicate bronze. *See, Babydoll. Nothin' to it. Come here and give Grandma a kiss.* Her crooked hands smelling of butter cupped my face. Only I saw the roll of my mother's watery eyes.

I REMEMBER

I remember the paneled walls, the rustled sheets of my bed, and the look on Ryan's face as he walked in small circles around my college bedroom. I was in a mid-drift and miniskirt, my belly tan for late April. We were nineteen. We were babies. And I had a paper to turn in for British Literature.

I remember the nausea coming in strong waves—sometimes in the morning, but mostly after classes. The doctor at Planned Parenthood suggested saltines and decaffeinated tea as she sat with me on the street curb, one hand on my back, the other drying my face.

I remember walking back in the building, sitting in her office, and listening, listening, listening—waiting for the answer I wanted. Waiting for the news that there had been a mistake. Waiting for her to release me so that I could puke up the coffee I apparently was not supposed to drink.

I remember a black and white picture in one of my anthologies of Sylvia Plath holding her daughter—a little bundle nestled against her, the baby's mouth slightly open. Even with her eyes closed, she looked like she had something to say.

I remember walking back into my little rented house, my roommates trying not to stare at my concave stomach. Wanting to ask questions. Wanting to leave me alone. Wanting to pee on sticks themselves. We were little girls playing house—little girls of all different majors, with an incessant hunger for meaning and truth. Lisa got the pillows, Jenna boiled water for tea, Sarah stepped onto the back porch to take a hit of pot. *You know, my nerves.* I nodded. We sat on the couch, silent, watching unremembered movies that day, braiding each other's hair, trying not to notice the three separate booklets I tossed on the beat-up coffee table, trying not to notice each other's eyes.

I remember my mother throwing the phone as the words spilled from my mouth—screaming in the background that my life was over. My dad picked up the receiver, panicked, readying himself. *Oh, okay. Shhhh. I thought something was really wrong. Something really bad.* These will always be the sweetest words my dad ever said to me.

I remember being so in love, a complete immersion in another person, confident that nobody in the entire world could possibly have what we had, feel what we felt. Almost two years after meeting, the butterflies were still there. My heart actually jumped, and I sometimes forgot to eat. We could read each other's minds from across the room of a

crowded frat party. *I've had enough of this tonight. Haven't you?*
Want to get out of here? Agreed. Smile. Smile. Blush. Exit. It
was a love so magical that a birth control pill could not
contain it, that the universe was speaking directly to me
saying I was still okay. I was still smart. I could contend
with the stigma because this is what was supposed to
happen. Right? This was the force I prayed to, cursed, and
doubted giving me a nudge, a sign. Right? I set logic aside
and listened to the butterflies in between the waves of
retching. I had discovered a glitch in the system—a tiny
wrinkle in time and space carved out especially for us.

I remember sitting in my psychology final, trying not to
notice Ryan glancing over at me between each question he
answered. Around and around my finger, I turned the little
pearl ring he had given me for Christmas. It was too big, so
I had tied some yarn around it to ensure it wouldn't fall off
my bony finger.

I remember whispering in my big sister's ear at our
Alpha Xi Delta chapter meeting. *I'm not coming back. I'm not*
getting an abortion. She reached for my hand, squeezing it
tight, tears brimming in her eyes. *This doesn't sound like you.*
I have to say it. It doesn't.

I remember cupping her face. *I know.*

I remember that summer. I was a nanny to a toddler
with hydrocephalus. I fed him, changed him, and rocked
him to sleep praying to God to please give me a healthy
baby.

I remember the whispers, the looks in the grocery store,

the questions my best friends endured. *Is it true? Is she really knocked up?* The walls of my former high school closed in, and my buried teen insecurities rushed back. The need to be thin, the need to fit in, the need for boys to notice me.

I remember seeing my geometry teacher at Blockbuster. He stared at my small stomach, I stared at his bald head and perpetually sneered face. I walked to my car promising myself that I'd always be kinder to young people than that fucker.

I remember hiding at home, deciding to befriend my mother, and eating Genaurdi's lemon crunch pie almost every night.

I remember my best friend, Cara, going to my first doctor's appointment with me. She didn't know what she was doing. I didn't know what I was doing. But we held our breath and we held hands and we stared at the glowing black and white screen as the tech said, *that is one strong heartbeat.*

I remember Ryan driving across the state to bring me to Pittsburgh and look in my mother's eyes as she forced out, *Call when you get there, ok?*

I remember smoothing two towels on the bed, right where my butt resided each night, hoping he wouldn't notice. I didn't want to be embarrassed anymore. It was bad enough that the body I needed to be skinny all my life had turned into this soft, vast mountain of flesh with a dark alien line running the length of my belly. My ankles looked like they belonged to a stranger. I was the epitome of unsexiness. I wanted my body back—to have some control over something. And goddammit, I was going to catch all of the fucking fluid when my water broke.

I remember Ryan turning on the *Tonight Show* and drawing back the comforter. *Do you know there are two towels here?* I felt myself flushing, but he let me keep my secret, and helped me onto the high bed without a mention of the towels.

I remember reading all of Shakespeare's works, promising myself to finish, writing notes in the margins of the tissue-thin Norton pages, doodling along the edges of *Romeo and Juliet.*

I remember coughing for days. Between my grandmother dying of cancer two weeks prior and the incessant Pittsburgh snow that bombarded our lives, I was not taking very good care of myself, but convinced my mother I was. The cough was deep, resonating through the house like the sound of an old smoker. *You can't take anything stronger. I'm sorry.* My doctor's answer to everything was *Tylenol*, which I convinced myself was a placebo invented to keep pregnant women uncomfortable—a part of a greater conspiracy promoted by the male medical community to control the population. The little white pills mocked me, my head pounding into a migraine with each reverberating cough.

I remember Ryan rubbing Vicks into my chest. He had no idea what to do. I had no idea what to tell him. We just waited. He completed his classes for the semester. He got all A's.

I remember the house smelled of cinnamon and vanilla. It was almost Christmas.

I remember my water breaking and waking me. It wasn't a huge gush like in the movies, and I caught it with the towels. *Ryan. I think this baby is coming.* I didn't move for fear of a second-wave gush. He was curled next to me on his side, his arm draped over my pillow. I remember thinking how gorgeous he was. How I hoped my baby looked just like him. How I hoped my baby had his heart. He groggily opened his eyes and smiled, moving his hand to my body to touch me, and then bolted upright, jumping straight off the bed, only to crawl back next to me. *Does it hurt?* I shook my head, and he lifted me to the floor.

I remember being sent home, three times. They told me my water didn't break; it was just a leak. And my painful contractions weren't really contractions.

I remember crying and coughing upon my last arrival and helping myself to a wheelchair. I demanded an epidural. I told them my pain was far worse than normal. The nightshift nurses looked amused. *You mean worse than all of the other pregnant women… ever?*

I remember Ryan stepping forward and grabbing a clipboard and pen. *Yes. That is exactly what she means.*

I remember the needle penetrating my back, sinking deep into my spine. *Don't move. Shhh. You are going to feel awesome in three, two, one.* Everything released. A floating rush travelled straight to my head, and I closed my eyes welcoming the greatest high ever. *I gave you a little narcotic in there too so you're going to feel pretty good for a while. See, look at this monitor. You're having a contraction.* The glowing line jumped and peaked. We laughed. The baby moved—a sharp elbow right to my ribs. I hugged the anesthesiologist and asked her to come to my wedding.

I remember each of the nurses, from all three shifts. Labor was slow, I was thirsty. They gave me ice chips, but that didn't help. Ryan melted them on the heater for me.

I remember his parents entering the room, his mother kissing my forehead and stroking my hair. She smelled like the same Estée Lauder perfume my mother wore, but still, it was different. I wanted my own mother, but wouldn't admit it. This wasn't the same.

I remember my hot doctor arriving, holding my hand. He looked like he belonged on a hospital TV show. *We're going to speed things up with Pitocin, okay? You'll be pushing soon.* I asked him to come closer. I told him I had a secret. *I don't think this baby is going to come out of such a tiny hole.* I put my hand over my mouth, stifling a cry that lodged in my throat. He smiled and touched my cheek. *Sure it will. Wait until you see how miraculous your body is. You're a lot stronger than you think.*

I remember being rolled into the delivery room, Ryan meeting me with scrubs on, and I didn't like the cap he had to wear. *Think he can take it off? It just doesn't look like him.* The next contraction came, and my body felt like it had been split in two. I forgot to care what he looked like. I forgot to care about a lot of things—my sadness over my parents' long drive from D.C., who was looking at or touching my body, or if I would shit on the table. It all faded into another existence as I pushed a human out of me. *You did it, and it's a boy.* The doctor placed the shrieking baby on my belly, and I repeated, *I did it. I did it. I did it.* Ryan took off the scrub cap, kissing my head, and then walked in circles with his hands in his hair. *Oh my God, I can't believe that just happened. You are so fucking amazing.*

I remember Ryan cutting the cord, even though he told me for nine months that he wouldn't.

I remember talking to this baby as he wailed, his nose smashed to the side of his face. The nurse read my mind. *Don't worry, honey. His nose will be fine tomorrow.* His cries grew softer and softer with each word I uttered. I remember how he looked straight into my eyes as I kept on babbling. I said whatever came to mind. I had been waiting for him for nine months, and I had so much to tell him—that I would try not to screw this up, that I actually pushed him out of me even though I didn't think I could, that I was sorry for not eating more vegetables, that I already had Christmas presents wrapped under the tree for him, that I would read him every book I owned, that I loved him already. The incredible being stopped crying and watched my mouth. *Jen, he knows you. Oh my God, look at his face. He's staring at you. He knows you.*

I remember these moments existing in a parallel universe where everything moves in slow motion. When Evan left my body, the entire world sped up like so much water rushing through my fingers. There was never enough time. For anything. Except burying the teen mom cloak that clung to me.

IN LOCO PARENTIS [1]

The alarm clock screamed for the third time, and I finally turned it off. Late, again, and with cramps. I blindly made my way to the bathroom, tripping over my dog, ramming my shoulder in the dresser. I knew I should have gone to the store; I knew this would happen. Another month gone by. Was I relieved or sad? Cramps or morning sickness? I was too exhausted to decide. I rummaged through the absurd clutter of my vanity drawer and found the box—a sample package holding (please, let it be a super-plus... please, let it be a super-plus) the last "lite" Tampax Pearl. *Jesus*.

I thanked the gods of frazzled teachers for the last-minute shower I took before crashing into bed the night before. It was a rough one filled with senior gradation project grades, final essays, and an exorbitant amount of cookie dough ice cream. I had managed about three hours

1 From Merriam-Webster's Dictionary:
*/lōkō pə'rentəs/adverb & adjective (of a teacher or other adult responsible for children) in the place of a parent. "She was used to **acting in loco parentis**."*

of sleep. Deodorant applied, ponytail secured, clothes wrinkled, but on, and tampon designed for a Barbie doll in place, I embarked on my last day with my seniors. It was their final exam, and I needed summer. Badly.

After dropping Evan off at school, I pulled into my parking spot, and rushed to the front doors expecting to meet my building principal with a quick "sorry," but once again the gods smiled upon me. No Jonathan. I gave myself an inner-monologue high-five and merged into the crowd of tired high schoolers trying to start their day.

"Ms. Rieger, we're in the cafeteria for the exam, right?"

"We need a #2 pencil, right?"

"Wait, are there essays? Can I use pen?"

Head down, I walked with a purpose, racing past students with whom I would normally hold a civilized conversation. I was a woman on a mission: Get to my desk drawer of normal sized tampons as quickly as humanly possible and make my way to the bathroom. I bumped into Kim, my 12th grade counter-part, and she looked concerned. "They're calling all faculty and staff into the LGI for a meeting," she whispered. Of course they are, of course it would be today, and...*wait*. The last time we were called together like this, a student had died. My pulse raced, and I started to sweat. We made our way to the large group instruction room and were greeted by our principals, township police, and the head of school security.

Administration passed copies of a photograph around, and I held in my hands the face of one of my graduates—a boy I had taught, laughed with, and cared for the previous year. He had been threatening our students over social media, and we were instructed to be vigilant. The surreal nature of the message somehow got lost in my already disheveled brain. This was not a scary kid. This was an overreaction. They had to respond like this to cover their asses. I made every kind of justification possible to process this new information. After all, I had a test to give. My kids were waiting for me.

Glancing at the clock, I knew I didn't have time to get to my classroom. I ran to the faculty bathroom, wadded up a ball of toilet paper, shoved it in my crotch, and washed my hands. It would have to do. Besides, I could slip out for a minute once we had the exams distributed. Kim, and the assistant principals helping us, would be able to keep an eye on things.

The cafeteria is the center of the high school. Like the building itself, it shows its age; however, the surrounding encased windows let in much needed natural light. That morning, the usually animated space closely resembled a slow-moving tornado of exhaustion and anxiety. "Please separate, little friends. No need to sit on each other's laps for the exam." We made our way around the cafeteria, moving students. *Where are the assistant principals?* I wondered. The kids were grouchy. At this point, like us, they just wanted out.

We distributed tests and scantrons through the miasma of whispers, but were quickly interrupted by the buzzing of the PA system. "The building is in lockdown. I repeat, the building is in lockdown." It was the voice of our main office secretary, that was clear; however, this was not the phrase that was taught to us in countless other preparation drills. Kim and I looked at each other over the blank stares of 200 teenagers. This was not a part of our training. Then a crying, cracking voice followed. "Dr. Emory. You are wanted in E-102."

And there it was.

There haven't been many instances in my life when time has stopped. When everything I've been taught or everything I've seen, read, or felt collides at the exact same moment. I wouldn't say it was my entire life that flashed through my mind, but an explosion of sporadic snippets of everything either directly or indirectly pertaining to that moment: My son playing the guitar, our in-service intruder drill instruction, my students' funny *Canterbury Tales* videos; my husband stroking my hair, meeting my best friend in the English office, one of my kids showing me his college acceptance letter, the disastrous clutter left on my classroom desk, my mom and dad at the beach, the image of the boy passed around that morning, and the Columbine hallways… the Columbine evacuation…the Columbine interviews… the Columbine cafeteria…the Columbine shooters.

I know it was only a few seconds. Kim told me later that it was only a few seconds, but it felt like I stood there forever before she snapped me out of it. She looked me square in the face, "This isn't a drill." For a split second, my eyes started to water. Kim grabbed my arm. "No." It was all she said, and I was back from my thoughts—back from fear. Kim grew up in South Africa and, on most days, possessed a fragile, sensitive heart. On this day, I learned of her logical stoicism. We were the parents at that moment— the responsible ones. No matter how hard I tried to conjure a more experienced teacher, someone resembling my own parents, the truth remained. We were the only two teachers in a cafeteria surrounded by glass containing over 200 of other people's children.

Principals and janitors locked the doors of the cafeteria, students ran in the hallways, and seniors were looking to me with questioning eyes. *What's going on? Who's the idiot that decided to have an intruder drill during a final exam? What are we supposed to do?* Only, I didn't know what we were supposed to do. I only knew what to do in my classroom. I looked to the snack bar area that had a garage-like rolling door. Would that be best? Hiding in there? I looked to the tables. Should we barricade in a corner? Something clicked and at the same time that I started yelling for kids to crouch under the tables in the middle of the cafeteria, our assistant principal was knocking on the glass screaming the same thing. "Under the tables, kids. Under the tables." A wave of nausea came over me. I had heard that same scream, that same repetition of words strung together, on the news, eight years before.

"Why are we in the middle? This is so stupid. It's only a drill anyway." And there presented our first problem. Sean Jefferies. He wasn't my student; he was Kim's. Sean was full of piss and fire. I had seen him at his kindest and at his meanest. He was a big kid—a football player—who relished his senior ownership over the high school hallways. He had many friends, but I saw how some of his classmates and teammates grew tired with his blowhard nature over the past twelve years. Look up any teen movie with the loud, smart ass, and you have your Sean archetype. "Under this table, Sean. Next to me. Now." Kim's eyes pierced through this giant man-child who gave her so much trouble that year. He sat, but a stone-throw away from her.

Some students were crying, some laughing like they were a part of a great joke, some intently texting their parents, some just staring blankly, eerily at the surrounding glass. "Psst. Ms. Rieger. My mom wants to talk to you." The little girl who sat in my tenth period each day was a mess of tears. I reached over and wiped them from her face. "Shhh." I reminded her that we had to stay silent, to whisper to her mom that she was okay and put her phone down. Was that the right response? Was that what I was supposed to say? Had I ever touched a student's face, let alone tears before? Was I supposed to? My brain felt like a file cabinet of information. Everything that I was ever taught or warned about was tucked neatly away, waiting for a moment's recall to thumb through and pick it up. I suddenly feared choosing the wrong file.

We sat. All sense of time was a mystery. The clock said we were only under the tables for ten minutes at that point, but wasn't it more like an hour? I dodged so many questions, provided a safe response of, "Whether it's a drill or not, our job is to stay here, silent." We calmed them down, we made some of them smile—and then the SWAT team showed up. Officers in full gear and machine guns ran through the halls on both sides of cafeteria towards the direction of the E-wing, and our newly calmed seniors lost it. "Okay. So now we know for sure it's not a drill. But we're staying here, silently. Shhh." Friends held onto each other and whispers of retaliation plans started.

But that's when Sean emerged.

"You can't make me stay here. I'm bouncing. I'm totally bouncing." His face was red. He looked like an oversized toy ready to spring to action.

"You're not 'bouncing.' You're going to sit there and, Sean, you will shut up," I said sternly, but calmly. I wanted to smack him. I wanted to hug him.

"I don't have to listen to you. I'll do what I fucking want. And I'm not staying here." Sean scanned the cafeteria for every possible exit.

While Sean looked for a place to run, Ryan Neufer and Brad Leonard, two of the biggest goofballs I had ever taught, were devising plans of their own. I had heard them whispering for a while—strategizing the best possible response for shielding their classmates with tables and attacking the intruder themselves. "Listen, everybody. If someone comes in here, do not run into the courtyard. You'll be trapped. We are going to rush him, and you all run for the hallways." At first it was a white noise, a low-talking drowned within the humming vending machines, but then I became acutely aware that these boys were serious. They were ready to defend their friends and themselves. They were ready to fight.

"Yeah. I'm out," Sean squatted next to the pillar, ready to run, when Ryan spoke up.

"I don't think you're going anywhere. I think you're going to listen to Ms. Rieger. Sit down and shut the fuck up. We're all tired of your mouth." Ryan's face suddenly possessed the countenance of an adult. Brad's typical baby face looked the same. I had never seen those two boys look so serious. Not during tests and quizzes, not even during their senior graduation projects. They had the air of young heroes, and I was in awe.

We sat. It was one of those spans of twenty-five minutes that felt like three hours. Sean held his head between his knees, Ryan and Brad remained vigilant, and some students started praying. I swallowed the lump in my throat that was slowly trying to suffocate me. "Kim," I whispered, "I think I might be sick." Kim grabbed my arm, "Swallow it down. You can be sick later. And sit on your hands." I looked down and my hands were involuntarily shaking. They looked older, somehow. Like they belonged to someone else. Like they belonged to my mother. How long had they been shaking like that? Did the kids see? I obeyed her instructions and looked around at my kids, smiling, reassuring them that the quiet from the hallways was a good sign—that we might have to sit there as a part of protocol. No sooner had I said that and an officer stood at the hallway window and put his hand on the glass. There were sudden whispers, "What does that mean? What does that mean?" With an air of confidence, I assured them that it meant the situation was under control, but that we were to stay put.

Kim whispered in my ear, "Is that what it really means?"

I mumbled, "Hell if I know."

I hunched under that table wondering how I got to this point. Wasn't I supposed to be a writer, rubbing elbows at poetry conferences with Mary Ruefle and Kim Addonizio? Wasn't I supposed to be spending these late spring months at retreats wearing woven island commune hippie clothes designed by women named Star? Having Evan changed all that. This was a direction I never expected. This is supposed to be the meantime—teaching in a public school so that I could make money, get my graduate degrees, and move on to my real calling. The one where I learn, create, and publish. The one where I'm not huddled under standard issue cafeteria tables contemplating the best place to run when gunfire broke out. The one where somebody else is responsible for the welfare of these children surrounding me. The one where I don't give a shit.

In the five minutes it took for the officer to come back, we had settled. Just a little. Unlocking the cafeteria door, the officer approached, telling us we could all stand up. "You know, I couldn't even see you in here. You did exactly the right thing." He told us what he could. A person had made threats the night before. He came into the building to intimidate, and now he was apprehended. This was now considered a crime scene, and we had to leave everything as it was and exit the building.

I stood to escort my students down to the football field, and that's when I felt the pool between my thighs, sopping the crotch of my pants and the small, but recognizable spot of blood where I had sat on the cafeteria floor. With my sandal, I wiped out the trivial reminder, not caring if anyone saw. All I wanted was to get them to the field—I knew their parents would be waiting. All I wanted was to run home and hold my own son.

The next day, my seniors returned to the cafeteria. I was conflicted about this decision. The mom in me wanted to tell our principal to forget about the final, to give them all A's and not make them enter that cafeteria ever again. The teacher in me knew he was probably right—we had to start a new day and not let outsiders control us. This was the plan; we would see it through. Rummaging through the great file cabinet in my brain, that was the file I chose. I was ready to defend the school's decision, to uphold academic integrity, but interestingly enough, none of my kids complained. They sat staggered at the lunch tables, pencils sharpened, ready to work. They were resilient. I was proud. I walked about the cafeteria touching each one that morning, even the ones that weren't mine. A pat on the shoulder, a rustle of their hair, a brief hug. I'm sure some thought I was crazy or slightly melodramatic; others have moms just like me and looked up with appreciation. Either way, I didn't care. They were safe and they were mine. All of them.

CURSE, BLESS ME

It was a day of back-to-back college essay conferences and my AP students were particularly needy. It was one of those days when "Ms. Rieger" merges into one word— Misreeger—and then gets repeated approximately one-thousand times. College deadlines were fast approaching, and I was charged with healing the woes of the colloquial and the hearts of the insecure.

After checking my phone during my prep period, I noticed a Facebook message from George, a student who had graduated two years prior. "Give me a call when you have a minute," and then his cell number. I didn't think too much of it; George would contact me on occasion. He was incredibly philosophical and liked to give me updates on new poetry and books he encountered. I knew he craved that academic connection and missed a traditional class.

George's life wasn't easy. His parents were both drug addicts and held long criminal records. He lived in an orphanage, twice, and had been left alone for days as a toddler. When his grandparents found him, he was malnourished and in the same diaper for days. They took him in and raised him as their own. To ask him, he'd say that he witnessed, firsthand, the benevolence of mankind and the ugliness of mankind at a very young age. He spent his middle school years in a delinquent facility. Lacking motivation and confidence, he occasionally had to kick the asses of bullies who loved to remind him that he was overweight. But high school changed a lot for him. Even though he struggled in some classes, he embraced the education he had been missing. He stepped out of his comfort zone; wrestled; actively trained in jiu-jitsu; embraced epics about honor, strength and courage; and decided that if I said poetry was awesome, he'd give it a try.

His favorite poem was Dylan Thomas's "Do Not Go Gentle into that Good Night." He loved it so much in fact, that he made the stretch to connect it to every single thing we read. Upon his graduation, he asked me to look after his friend, Branden, who was two years younger than him—a boy in my own son's class. I promised I would, and sure enough, Branden's name appeared the following year on my eleventh grade roster.

Branden was not an easy child. He was among the most lovable students I had ever taught, but he was also among the laziest. George knew I had my work cut out for me and even said, "Hit him with that 'mom look' you've got going on. That kills everyone, and you're really fucking good at it."[2] I was indeed really fucking good at it. Every time something was due, and Branden averted his eyes, I laid it on thick. "I mean, Branden, it's not that I'm mad that you don't have your homework. I'm just…disappointed. Am I boring? Is there something else I can do to hold your attention? I don't know. Just wondering if this is somehow *my fault*." Spell cast. Branden hung his head, fidgeted with his hands, and finally looked at me. "God. I'm such a dick." I'd sigh, walk away, and he'd have a full draft of his paper in my inbox that night, letting me know I was a good teacher, and I should never blame myself. Sorcery perfected.

From the very first day of school, Branden kept asking, "When are we going to read that poem George keeps talking about?" Obviously, anything George loved was okay in Branden's book. Although the poem is on the twelfth grade curriculum, I printed it out for Branden, told him to read it, and walked away certain that poor Dylan Thomas was destined for a crumbled horror at the bottom of Branden's book bag. Much to my surprise, he came back the next day with notes scribbled all over it. He was excited and wanted to discuss. So we did. He was amazed by it all: the villanelle's repetition, the parallel structure indicative

2 The "mom look" is among a few of my superpowers. My students can feel it searing into the backs of their little heads from the far seats of a crowded auditorium whenever they're acting like fools. They can also sense it as they tell me of "printer problems" when an essay is due, when the assistant principal calls them out of my class, and when they run to bathroom with the speed of Jackie Joyner-Kersee whenever I ask for a volunteer to read aloud. The "mom look" has the power to propel with lightning speed the most apathetic student right from my senior project podium, through the mainline roads of Montgomery County, and onto the graduation stage at Villanova University. I should charge a fee.

of all men, the way the form of the poem itself signified a perpetual rebirth. He promised to make me proud in twelfth grade English when he read it again.

Kicking and screaming the whole way, Branden moved on to twelfth grade. He found himself in my best friend Rachel Darnell's class. With English as the only four-year required course, she was deemed the gatekeeper of Branden's diploma. We both knew that Rachel would love him, but she also had a unique mom-look of her own and was not going to take any of his shit. She pulled him through the college essay, through the literature, and finally through the senior graduation project. His stellar moment was impressing her with his knowledge of "Do Not Go Gentle," and then finally raged against the dying of the light all the way across the stage at graduation.

I replied to George's message. No answer. While I don't normally give my number to students, I had a feeling I should. Hitting send, I shook the message from my mind, and finished out the day. By 2:21, I had four missed phone calls and one message. "Riegs, this is George. Branden was hit by a van. It's bad. I don't think he's going to make it."

Branden spent the majority of his time body building. He would meet George at the gym and lift, contemplate life, and talk shit. He told his mother that he was training for the fight of his life. His doctors would agree. When the van hit him, it was like hitting a tank, except that tank's motherboard couldn't withstand the blow. That drunk driver literally knocked Branden from his sneakers, and he flew.

"Riegs, do you think you could get here? I'm at Penn University Hospital."

I thought of this young philosopher—the boy who wrote about heroes, strength, and honor. The boy who spent his entire education searching for a mom to care for him when he needed one.

"George, I'm not great in those situations. I don't know if I can hold it together."

My voice cracked, and he whispered into the phone, "Shhh. It's okay. I understand."

I said goodbye and started packing up my things. A wave of nausea hit me as I walked down the back stairwell. I paused at the bottom, holding onto the cinderblock wall. I stared at the screen of my phone—at the messages I had missed from him that day. I touched his name and typed. *George. I'll be there within the hour. Tell me where you are.* I sent the text, and headed to my Jeep.

The traffic along the Schuylkill Expressway was thick. I later discovered that there was an accident causing the gridlock, and I couldn't make my way around it. I dialed. "George, I can't get there." He told me he understood, that he wasn't sure if Branden could hear anyone anyway. "Do me a favor, George. Google 'Do Not Go Gentle' and read it to him. At the end, exchange the word 'father' for 'brother.' George? Do you understand?" I heard a faint "yeah," and some muted whispers in the background, and then he started to read, "Do not go gentle into that good night, old age should burn and rave at close of day; Rage, rage against the dying of the light." He continued, with an excellent cadence and momentum that would make any teacher proud. When he came to the line, "And you, my brother, there on that sad height," there was a pause, then a gasp, and then he started repeating over and over, "He's moving his hands! Ms. Rieger! He's moving his hands!"

Whenever tragedy strikes our school community, Rachel and I make a plan. It's what we do. We headed to Penn a few days later to stare at the pummeled, broken shell of the boy we constantly pushed, constantly questioned, constantly guilted. We looked at the worn face of his young mother, Tammy, my age, who had already lost a child to cancer. We had collected enough money from the faculty and staff to get Branden an iPad. I don't know why. I think the purchase meant that we could will him to open his eyes, watch the screen, listen to the music. Holding the box, Tammy tilted her head to the side and nodded as her eyes welled and her voice shook, "Yes. He will like this very much. He will use it all the time." I knew this mother didn't need any more tears, but a quick sob escaped my throat. Rachel, as solid as ever, grabbed my arm and we allowed Tammy to talk to the doctors. We eavesdropped for a few moments as they updated her on Branden's condition. It didn't sound good. Medical terminology floated among the beeping of machines, the pumping of the ventilator, and shuffling of hallway activity. Words repeated, "pressure," "fluid," and "surgery." Rachel and I nodded as if we knew what the hell they were talking about. After a few minutes, his dad, Allen, walked in. Tammy sighed, fell into him, like she had been carrying a bag full of weights all day, and managed to convey the doctors' update. Looking over her shoulder, she said to us, "He's a 'whisperer,' you know. I don't know how he does it." Allen leaned on the bed, and began massaging Branden's arms and legs, whispering in his ear. "Shhh. How's that, my man? Lots of people here Branden. Your English teachers are here. They say you owe them some work. They're waiting for you to wake up and smile." Rachel and I stood, glued to one another—our nails pressed into each other's hands. We could only handle our uncomfortable family intrusion a few minutes more. We hugged this couple—this pillar of strength and sadness—walked a few paces down the hall, and broke down in front of the elevator.

We were silent on the ride back.

"How many more times do you think we'll have to do this, Rach? I mean, the hospitals and the funerals? Twenty more times? Thirty?"

"I don't know. I can't get Tammy's face out of my head. She's everywhere."

I unfastened my seat belt, grabbed her hand, and kissed it. "That's because we're her." I stepped out of her minivan and entered my house through the garage door. It would be quiet. Ryan was out of town, and Evan was at school. I had noticed he posted a video on Branden's Facebook page. He gathered three friends and recorded "May the Good Lord Bless and Keep You." He knew the hymn would comfort that mother—knew it would lighten his own mother's heart. My child. Safe, in his dorm room.

I called George as soon as I entered the house. We discussed all the big questions of "why." Why did this happen to Branden? Why would a family, already destined to mourn a daughter for the rest of their lives, have to endure yet another tragedy? Why are there really horrible people, real assholes, who get to roam the earth unscathed? If we must endure pain, why isn't it equally distributed? Some answers were beautiful and comforting; others were ugly and appalling. I asked George what Dylan Thomas's lines, "Curse, bless me, with these fierce tears, I pray," meant to him.

"Well," George began, "he's trying to grasp death—this ending we all have to face, eventually."

I agreed, but prodded a little more. "George, why are endings, why are tragedies, a blessing and a curse?"

He had heard the question before, as a student in my English class, sitting in the desk perfectly adjacent to my own desk. There was silence on the other end. I'm used to this with him. He processes and thinks about his words carefully before speaking.

"It's a curse because it really sucks. Times like this fucking suck. And it's not fair." I stopped him before he went any further.

"Why is it a blessing, George?" Again silence.

"I don't know," he finely said.

"Yes you do," I quickly retorted. The volume of my voice increased, and I slowed my words down. "Why- a- blessing?"

His voice cracked, "Because I'm sitting here on the

phone with my English teacher, contemplating time, and appreciating what I have."

Branden did improve, but the after-effects of his brain injury are pretty extensive—something he will always contend with. His mom and dad care for him, love him, advocate for him. The last I saw him was at a bowling fundraiser. George and I met there wearing Captain America shirts—a community symbol for Branden's strength. As soon as we walked up to his wheelchair, he smiled, and reached his arms up to hug us. "You're my brother," he managed to slowly say to George. "That's right, brother. Always." Branden looked to me, and struggled with his words. "And you and Ms. Darnell are my moms." Just like Rachel did in that hospital room, George grabbed my arm. As I looked at this child's now drawn face, now crooked smile, now dented skull, I nodded emphatically. "You're right, Branden. Always."

That night, George and I drank shitty bowling alley beer and bowled our hearts out. We talked about Nietzsche and *Beowulf*, and sent pictures to his own 2010 classmates. It was like nothing had changed, and everything had changed. Every once in a while, we'd look over at Branden, greeting his guests. We'd catch each other's eyes, but there were no words left.

Grow

Ancient Egyptians used sage as a remedy for infertility. It was also a main embalming ingredient.

THE UNDERTAKING

We all know that something is eternal. And it ain't houses and it ain't names, and it ain't earth, and it ain't even the stars . . . everybody knows in their bones that something is eternal, and that something has to do with human beings. All the greatest people ever lived have been telling us that for five thousand years and yet you'd be surprised how people are always losing hold of it.

—Thornton Wilder, *Our Town*, Act III

"I'll get it," I yelled, charging toward the out-of-bounds kickball. My legs moved with precision, but the tiny stone memorial caused me to freeze, almost as if someone had just pressed pause on our home VCR. Near the giant maple tree, two little handprints were etched with a simplistic script underneath of *Emma White 1964–1972*. The ball kept rolling, but I kept my silence, immobile in the sacred spot that my fourth-grade classmates casually passed each day.

For a long time, I thought poor Emma's body was buried there, but I learned that it was just a memorial—a small gesture to honor a fallen Longwood Elementary School Lion. I'd often pay my respects to this little girl, sometimes during a solitary stroll during cold Chicago winter recesses, sometimes making my way to the tree during a game of tag. I would discreetly match my own hands with the cool stone, thinking of the girl who once sat on the same swings, dangled from the same monkey bars, and jumped on the same hopscotch squares. To me, Emma White's surreal existence was similar to canonized saints—they were here once, there's evidence to support that. But to actually consider this fact bordered on the realm of fantastical—a beautiful, spiritual wonderment exceeding my own reality of Barbies, Saturday morning cartoons, and sticker collections. One day I even garnered the courage to ask my teacher about her.

"Mr. Day, did you know Emma White? What was she like?" Now, I am certain Mr. Day had heard that same question many times over the years, but as a naïve fourth grader, I was convinced I had asked him something incredibly profound. He looked down at me for an instant, his gray hair falling to his eyes, took off his glasses, and wiped them with his handkerchief.

"Emma was a lot like you. She had blond hair like you, she had light brown eyes like you, and she liked to swing extra-high on the swings like you. I think the only difference is that Emma was a very, very sick little girl, and you are very healthy." I looked at Mr. Day's glassy eyes, and my throat tightened. I started to cry for his student, for the exquisite miniature handprints outside our classroom window, even for my classmates who didn't seem to give a damn that Emma White was once here in this room. It was too much for my dramatic, tender heart. Mr. Day wiped my face and told me that he was sure Emma would want me to play on the playground with the strength of two little girls. So I did just that.

In between school, dance class, and birthday parties, I would romanticize my own demise—succumbing to my own fatal illness like poor, little Emma White. What would my funeral look like? Who would weep uncontrollably? Could they add my name to Emma's sweet memorial under the maple tree? How disturbing! What was going on in my poor fourth grade existence? Any time a TV show or movie depicted a funeral, my eyes would fixate on the glowing screen in unabashed awe. The elegance of the ceremonious traditions, the handsome pallbearers, the somber procession, and the perfect flowers adding to my peculiar ideation of after-life mysteries.

Then, the summer before fifth grade, my grandfather died.

I wasn't close with my dad's father, but I liked him. For a man in his late 70s, he was incredibly active, which I guess was why everyone was so shocked when he died. Heart failure. My family was devastated; I was just scared. My Cresson summer activities came to a halt, and I began asking questions of my friends, read every encyclopedia I could get my hands on, searching for answers. Volume after volume, page after page—*heart failure (see also heart attack)*, *death, rigor mortis, decomposition, embalming, burial, cremation.* My mind delved into exceedingly gruesome, morbid places. My summertime friends, Cristy and Vicki, offered their own selfless assistance to my investigation. *What happens when you die?* We ran around town and surveyed aunts, uncles, cousins, friends to satisfy my quest for truth—the ugly realities adults spoke of in whispers. I had either known of or known personally some of "the dead," and the reverence paid to these departed souls only made my fascination with their memories all the more compelling: my great-grandfathers, my Aunt Marilyn's husband, my cousins— Chris and Denny—both tragically killed in automobile accidents. But I was little. Shielded.

Vicki was the first to offer an explanation. "Your body lies in a peaceful rest. Then Jesus flies down, captures your soul, and swoops you to heaven where everything is perfect. There are puffy, white clouds, and you get to see everyone who died before you. Even famous people. Even our dead dogs." Cristy peered at her younger cousin as if she was an embarrassing, genetic mutation in their brilliant family tree. She was, after all, an entire year older than us and, therefore, possessed far superior knowledge.

"Their bodies go stiff, and they poop and pee their pants. Then they are taken to Kennedy Funeral Home where Mr. Kennedy drains their blood, removes their organs to place in little clay jars, then stuffs them full of hay, and sews their mouths shut with a needle and thread. While this is happening, Miss Kennedy puts makeup on them. Yes, even the men. Oh, and they do all of this to them while they're naked." She placed her hand on my shoulder and shook her head. Cristy. The bearer of truth. I had tried to understand the advanced terminology in the encyclopedias, but what she said seemed to sum it up. Death sucked. And I had heard enough.

I wasn't allowed to go to my day camp. I wasn't allowed to go to the pool. I sat in my grandparents' tiny house on Cathedral Avenue, learned to play gin rummy by Leo, my grandparents' friend who, to this day, I remember being one of the sweetest souls I've ever encountered, and tried to decipher the whispers—tried to understand what it all meant. There is a beginning and there is an end, to everything. That seemed clear enough. It made me think of my field trip to an arboretum in third grade, and how our tour guide had explained that the life of a tree is a lot like the life of a human. They're born of seeds, develop roots to grow, suffer injury and disease, and eventually, age and die. But she then told us of the giant sequoias of the redwoods in California, and how some of them have lived for centuries upon centuries, and as I pondered this, it all seemed incredibly unfair. Compared to a sequoia, seventy-six years is nothing. I sat with my encyclopedia in the back corner of my grandma's bedroom, feeling small and insignificant, the fake wooden paneling of the walls not feeling like those giant trees in California. How I wanted to be there—lost among the natural world of the northwest coast, waiting for the slivers of light to peek through the leaves.

Walking into Kennedy's Funeral Home the night of the viewing was not the majestic ending to earthly life as depicted in movies. My grandfather looked like someone else. They forgot his glasses, he was in a suit and tie for God's sake, and his hands looked like they were from a Halloween costume store. Some people were crying softly, but others were just talking and laughing, like they were at the farmer's market on a bright summer day. Nobody told me I was going to see a dead body. Nobody told me that my PapPap was not going to look like my PapPap. I held my breath as my dad held onto my shoulder. His strong, but loving grip said, "I love you and this is awful, standing here. But this is what we do."

I walked out the front door of Kennedy's and sat under an inconspicuous tree by the hearse garage, not caring if my parents noticed that I had disappeared or if I messed up my stuffy church clothes. Underneath a blanket of stars on that hot, August night, I played with the dirt, drawing and clearing the same name over and over again.

CONFESSION

I sit the bottle of pinot noir at the edge of the sunken tub and lower my bloated body into the almost-scalding water. I didn't think to take a wine glass up with me.

Alcohol is a depressant. This isn't helping. My best friend's echo rattles my logic. It's decent wine—a Scott Paul Audrey Pinot Noir, named for Audrey Hepburn. I received it as a gift after completing my master's and kept holding off, waiting for the perfect moment to drink it.

I forgot the music. Forgot a towel. Even forgot the damn organic patchouli bubble bath to hide my protruding abdomen. *Too late now.* I bite the cork out of the bottle, spit-shoot it straight into the toilet, and swallow the liquid velvet. Still a tang to it with plum, a little spice. Each gulp soothes, warming my core to match my red, submerged skin. The knot in my throat releases—strand by intricate strand, balled nerves untangle the tiny, parallel cluster that formed as the tumor in my abdomen grew.

Balancing the bottle, closing my eyes, I sink. Chin, nose, eyes. I exhale five months of questions into tiny bubbles of exhaustion and regret. Tomorrow it will all be over. A window of procrastination shut. The Fates somewhere smiling, weaving my barren future into reality with the slice of the surgeon's scalpel. The extrication of my uterus. The stitched memory like a medieval tapestry.

I break the surface for a breath and a few more gulps. Yesterday's mascara burns my eyes, elicits tears. One more swallow. Okay, maybe another. My mind races over the past few years. Should I, or shouldn't I? To baby, or not to baby? Waiting for the right moment. Waiting for the perfect time in my career. Waiting.

The final sip spills from the bottle making a ribbon of maroon haze, and he walks in. Cork floating in the toilet, bottle floating in the bathtub, mascara blurring into the pink water. "You know you're not supposed to drink tonight." Ryan grabs a towel, lifts me from the water, pats me dry, and carries me to our bed.

"I waited too long," I finally say, after months of silencing the words.

"Shh. You're a mess," he whispers, drying my hair, wiping black rings from my eyes.

"I know. I am. I'm sorry."

ELEGY

If only I could nudge you from this sleep.

There's a raw and frankly heart-pulverizing poem by Theodore Roethke that's been circling in my mind for some time now called "Elegy for Jane." The sentiments of the speaker, a teacher, could very well match my own. Because it's an elegy and also begins with the subtitle, "My student, thrown from a horse," the outcome is clear. Once a sweet little "wren" flitting about, bringing joy and laughter into the lives around her, Jane left this world too soon. By the end, the poem shifts attention away from Jane and onto the speaker where he contemplates why he's standing at her fresh grave—what right does he have to mourn like this when he is neither a spouse nor a parent? He's just a teacher. And he's at a loss identifying these feelings.

The speaker may not understand, but I do. When I trained for this profession, nobody ever told me how much I would love them. Or that many will suffer unspeakable tragedies. Or that many will die.

I thought it would get easier, but it doesn't. On a warm, October evening, I stood at the casket of a man who died of a heroin overdose, but underneath the mask of the mortician's thick makeup, I saw a shadow of the boy who barreled into class ready to derail every lesson and charm me into, well, anything but British literature; the kid whose leg shook each football game day because he just couldn't wait to charge the field; the baseball player who screamed the lyrics of "Buttercup" and rallied the whole team, whether there was a win or a loss. My student. Gone.

Looking around the funeral home, there they were. My kids, only now with the faces of adults. So many approached, wondering if I remembered them. *Of course I do.* Some apologized for not keeping in touch. *It's okay.* Some apologized for treating me like shit all those years ago. *That's okay too.* I wanted their faces to comfort me, but they didn't. I steadied myself so as to not shake their shoulders and beg them to be safe—beg them not to be the next casket I cry over. Instead, I dried their eyes and cheeks with my sleeve. I held their faces remembering their carefree days of games, homecoming skits, and proms. Their older, wiser eyes looked like they had seen a lot. They were different eyes than the ones I dried at another funeral fifteen years before. Another classmate, another drug overdose. Dianna was sixteen, and my first student death.

It's a matter of numbers, really. The more students I

teach, the more likely I am to witness tragedy. But I'm over two decades in, and I'm tired. I'm tired of waking up on weekend mornings to see #RIP all over my social media. I'm tired of my kids getting hit by drunk drivers—suffering life-altering brain injuries and paralysis. I'm tired of motorcycle accidents, suicides, gunshots, and drug overdoses. I'm tired of the "Sad News" e-mails in my inbox from principals and counselors communicating yet another young death. I'm tired of the ugly skirt and sweater combo that I only wear to viewings and funerals. I'm tired of the days I sit in silence with my two best friends and colleagues, Rachel and Jason, staring at each other—three masters of language, silent. I'm tired of holding the hands of parents I once laughed with at Back-to-School Night, relaying my condolences, when I know they will never be complete again. Ever.

I'm tired. Just really tired.

The death of a child—a girl thrown from a horse or a boy unfairly stricken with a deadly virus—was once an unexpected tragedy that has morphed into ugly ritual. Heroin, suicide, drunk driving, guns—the march of our modern monsters. For decades they've crept into our lives; they take all that is precious, and they do not give back. This is our current reality. Emotions are not desensitized; I have my own stages of grief. The shock, the disbelief, the denial, the acceptance, the anger. I hear the news, sort through the e-mails, texts, and Facebook messages from my graduates, call Rachel and Jason—also shaken to the core because this is their kid too. We meet in the English office the next morning, walk into my room to stare at the collage of that particular graduating class, and make plans. Jason will drive, Rachel and I will wear our ugly funeral attire, we'll get coffee beforehand. We will immerse ourselves in our current students to ameliorate the sting and try to talk about anything else, all the while preparing ourselves. Another funeral home, another tiny card with a prayer or poem on the back, another casket filled with high school memorabilia. We stand together with reluctant acceptance, holding hands, staring at the plaster face of what was once our kid. This is what we do.

As Roethke points out, it's complicated. Teachers are charged with much more today than academic instruction. We become their caretakers and battle their monsters. We bear witness to their strengths and flaws that inevitably meld into this wondrous grey of reality. Graduation nights, we cheer as students who appeared to be lost causes graduate; we win over the passive-aggressive assholes who, by all accounts, end up not being assholes; we sit with ill parents who beg us to watch out for their kids if they should die; we hold the hands of pregnant girls who don't know where to turn; we cry with them over dead dogs, dead grandparents, feed them when there's no money for food, and dry their faces when they're forced to leave because, for many, our classrooms are the only places that ever felt like home.

So those who were taken far too soon—those whose lives were cut short—their ghosts linger. I'm a smart woman—I know how the blessing and curse cycle will work. I return to my classroom, my heart swells with gratitude for all the faces before me, I love them like my own, and pray for them to a God who I'm not even sure is listening to me anymore.

And then it will happen again. It's what they never tell you when you're completing the coursework in college, because if they did, nobody would do this job.

That night, I said goodbye to Albert. A man who left this world far too soon. Today I remember all the others: Dianna, Ben, Ashley, Seth, Buddy, Keith, Victor, Jess, Meghan, Linda, Jeff, James, Andre, Christina, Neil. Children who weren't mine, but also were—at least each for one year, forty-eight minutes every day.

THE FIX

Nestled in the back corner of my classroom, perfectly adjacent to my much nicer, high-back teacher chair, is a tattered, blue office chair. Before the chair's sad and shabby state, it lived in my extra bedroom, the room I temporarily deemed an "office," while patiently awaiting a whitewashed cradle, changing table, and pastel rocker that were never needed. The chair comforted me and took a beating as I immersed myself in the life of an English teacher and was transported from new house to new house before permanently residing here, in its cinderblock, academic abode.

It's a comfortable swivel chair—cushioned and adjustable, with just the right give for teenagers rocking themselves into a state of peaceful, if somewhat resistant, contentment. That chair has held students struggling with college essays, and students fighting with parents. It's heard stories of learning disabilities, failing grades, unexpected A's, and unplanned pregnancies. The dingy armrests and faded upholstery have supported the most confident and most vulnerable—those reveling in their teenage years and those contending with them.

Somehow, I became a mother to many of the chair's inhabitants. Give me a kid whose problems I could solve with the skills acquired through my English degrees, and I'll give you my new project. Family struggling financially? Have a seat and let's open a Google Doc—we're going to have fun writing scholarship essays. Math teacher giving you a hard time? Let me take a trip downstairs and schmooze him a bit. First love break your heart? I have tissues, chocolate, and a free afternoon of grading-procrastination. I hold their hands, wipe tears from their eyes and snot from their faces, and love them as my own. This is the side of teaching they don't tell you about—the side that makes the headaches, heartaches, and the dual caffeine-wine addiction worth it.

My own son spent many childhood years watching me compose research papers, literary analyses, and later, lesson plans in that very home office and from the tattered blue chair. He recently graduated from college with a degree in vocal performance, and he's trying to adjust to the life of a young, struggling artist. My husband Ryan and I, having had him at the oh-so-grown up age of nineteen, sometimes ponder from where this child came. He was a funny little kid of intellect and creativity, but also possessed an introverted nature that embraced the adult world, dismissing childhood frivolities.

As he got older, Evan became increasingly contemplative. He's a skeptic—a thinker and a worrier. He holds his cards close and most days you need a chisel and a pickaxe to reach his softer side. But, it's there. In moments of either sheer happiness or extreme disillusionment, when only a mom can suffice, he lets me in. And I love it. These moments are rare though, so when I come across students who I connect with, students who need me, students whose doubts and fears spill out from the safety of that chair, I can't help but make them my own.

I never believed I was supposed to be a mother. How I got pregnant in the first place, the odds were ridiculous! I don't know whether to laugh or cry when I hear of all the fertility treatments my friends have had to endure, when Ryan, in his dashing potency, barely sneezed on me and low and behold, it's a boy! As we juggled the new and peculiar responsibilities of young parenting in a sea of our own college antics and anxieties, we treated Evan as more of a sibling than our child. He attended concerts and parties with us, watched *Friends* and *Seinfeld* on Thursday nights, insisted on calling us Jen and Ryan during his entire second year of life, and learned to tap a keg at the age of three. Even in our youthful naiveté, he was loved, intellectually stimulated, and a tad spoiled; but I was also the mom who forgot about show and tell, felt frozen chicken nuggets qualified as a suitable dinner, and spent more time on my career than playing in the yard.

Despite our unconventional parenting style, Evan was still a sweet boy. I read everything to him, from Mother Goose to Shakespeare. He'd climb onto my lap as I worked, sucking his pacifier, curling my hair in his fingers, and ask me to read what I was writing. "Well, you see Evan, once upon a time there was an old king, King Lear, who really wanted people to tell him how great he was. Two of his daughters lied about how much they loved him so that they could get his land, but the third kind and lovely daughter remained loyal and true." His brown eyes would glance up to my face to gauge my seriousness. I'd wink, and he'd go back to weaving his chubby fingers through my hair.

My career progressed, and years of proving myself seemed to amalgamate along with many student faces. I devoted the majority of my time to them, whether it was helping with assignments, attending their games, or listening to their problems. I had to excel. I had to inspire. I had to change lives. Stigma is a funny thing. As much as I logically know that I succeeded—becoming a teacher, attaining graduate degrees and awards, becoming Department Chair—the whispers never really go away. When you spend years answering questions of people who think they're masters of inconspicuousness, but are really as transparent as cling wrap, you become quite good at detecting bullshit. *So, wait, what year did you graduate from high school? What year were you married? And Evan is, how old? Are you Catholic?* My colleagues, Ryan's colleagues, neighbors. Evan's friends' parents. Think I don't see your soul, Karen? Fuck you.

Time passed. At the age of thirty-four, I knew my window was closing. I knew if I wanted another baby, I couldn't wait. I read books, I talked to other mothers, I went off the pill. But instead of a baby, the doctors found a ten-pound tumor in my uterus—a mass slowly taking over my body and destroying a decision I had put off for years.

It hasn't been until recently when I started pondering that closed window once again, paying attention to this older body, hearing the whispers I've tried to block out—aged eggs that I still possess haunting me from the very ovaries I decided to keep when the surgeon took my uterus. I can hear them, small baby voices, ticking off every hour, every day, every year, trying so hard to team up with an errant sperm. Those baby ghosts love to whisper; they love to hypnotize me every time I smell a newborn's head or even look at Facebook posts of toddlers splashing in bathtubs and playing in pumpkin patches. But the truth is, those whispers are small echoes of a life that wasn't supposed to be—a life I unknowingly abandoned when I stepped foot in that classroom and used my time to care for other people's children. Those whispers taunt from some innate, ancestral, maybe even mystical place of wonder that, surely, I'll never understand. What I do understand is the transformative value—how to use those voices to repair others and bring meaning to my life. For every student rocking in that blue chair, I have purpose. Like my own grandmother's summers with me, I am able to correct the naïve transgressions of young motherhood with a kind of cosmic redo. I take in their doubts, their pain, their love, and relish their comfort and happiness when I console and dole out advice. They hug me, and thank me, and tell me that I'm the one who got them through.

If only they knew.

If only they knew that at night, when I contemplate all of my inevitable graduation goodbyes, all of my children that will leave me, I wind up curled in Ryan's arms. He strokes my hair, and reminds me that I'm loved, that there will be other kids who need me, that this isn't the end. If only they knew that in the dark hours of sleepless mornings, I sometimes find myself sitting in my home office, the room I had hoped would be a nursery, and I stare out the window thinking that while I do love my students, I'm no hero. I'm just a mom looking for a way to quiet the echoes.

RIDING SHOTGUN

Don't give up
You know it's never been easy
Don't give up
'Cause I believe there's a place
There's a place where we belong
—Peter Gabriel, "Don't Give Up"

A few years ago, I travelled to Salem, Massachusetts, for a poetry festival and, in a short time, became quite smitten with this historic little town—the crystals, the incense, the cemeteries, the witch lore. It has since become so dear to me that I fly or drive there whenever I need to be alone with my thoughts and my journal. Salem, for what was once a place imbued with the fiery stench of patriarchal control and punishment, is today rich with feminine power and, honestly, weirdness. I love it. My favorite town activity is perching myself in a corner at Gulu Gulu Café, journal open. I order a London Fog, if it's morning, an Allagash Triple if it's after, well, noon. I write about everything from Hester Prynne to the flowering trees up by Gallows Hill. I eat crepes and people-watch like it's my job. Every kind of person stops in for a drink—every kind of person Judge Hathorne would have sent to the gallows, myself included. That asshole had little tolerance for women, especially educated ones with an opinion. I spend days walking these old streets feeling energized, emboldened. Whatever literal, emotional, or spiritual work has taken place for centuries after the hangings, whatever mystical cleansing was performed to rid the cobblestones of men like Hathorne, you can feel it in the water and taste it in the air.

On this particular visit my friend, Rae, convinces me to see a medium. Rae is probably one of the coolest friends I've ever had. In a matter of minutes, she can change the energy of a room with her quick wit, and her keen knowledge of every witchy, magical, feel-good force field can make any skeptic curious. But she knows I'm not down with the idea. For one, I'm a believer in science. I like believing in science. It grounds me and tells me that even though there are questions out there that simply don't have answers, I'm okay. The world makes sense. I can sit in an empty church and ask God, or my ancestors, or the universe for guidance, but in the end, the answers are up to me.

The truth is, ever since I was little, every mystic, tarot reader, and magic shaman has tried to tell me that I was "special," "unique," and "possessed the sight." It scared me when I was younger. With the exception of a boardwalk fortuneteller who ripped me off in middle school, I've never participated in readings, Ouija Board gatherings, seances, or any other-worldly explorations. It's not that I'm a disbeliever. On the contrary, through the years, my curiosity has piqued. I've always been intuitive—sometimes uncomfortably so. And as I've gotten older, my sensitivities have only intensified. I can scan the faces of a classroom of students and feel the ones who are in pain. When I check homework, making my way around the room, my eyes will sometimes water from the force of their sadness. My friend Jeff, who teaches physics, has given me a very logical, very scientific reason for this.

"Jen, as you've taught more and more students, your brain has been busy cataloguing facial expressions. Any new encounter scans, accesses memory, and recalls the emotion."

The explanation makes sense, I just wonder about Jeff's response, if he could also feel how their sadness sets my skin on edge—tiny impulses that start at my arms and go straight to my throat.

Rae was a woman on a mission. "Oh, come on! It's cathartic," she says. There's something about this little poet-pixie friend of mine that could probably convince me to get drunk, skinny dip at Winter Beach, and then inhale a double brownie sundae. Thank God for small requests. So, I agree to the medium.

My appointment with Lauren was at 7:00 PM. Dusk felt appropriate. I sat in the Zen vestibule just outside the door and waited for Rae's appointment to end. The trickling waterfall onto a Buddha's belly made me wish I'd had peed. Rae exited, crying.

"Oh my God, what have you gotten me into? This can't be good!" I hugged her and she handed me a packet of tissues.

"I promise, they're good tears. I feel great. But you'll need these."

"Hi, Jen! I'm Lauren. Give me a minute to clear the space."

Her smile beamed, violet eyes pierced. If you could capture sunlight in a person, Lauren would be the vessel. From my side of the door, I could smell something familiar—something that took me back to long runs through grass, twilight and dinner bells. It was too crisp and clean to be weed, too earthy for incense. The door opened and Lauren invited me to take off my shoes.

"Thanks for being patient. Rae's session went a bit long, and I wanted to sage the room."

That was it. The herb I used to rub in my hands in my grandmother's yard. The smell of twilight and tradition. That leaf that grew wild with abundance. Historians said it was believed to cure, soothe, heal, and guide souls to another life, beyond the human pain of this world. I inhaled, remembering it all. Remembering childhood nights. And grandmothers. And Cresson.

"You sit, Jen. Begin to breathe and let go of the anxiety surrounding you." With the exception of typical end-of-the-school-year stressors, I didn't feel much anxiety. Just nostalgia and wonder.

We engaged in some small talk about the weather and the

poetry festival before she settled in. "Give me your hands." With only some slight skepticism I obliged, and Lauren inhaled and exhaled with intention. I naturally mimicked and soon our breath was in unison. She stared into my eyes. "Every so often I'll close my eyes, but I don't want you to break your gaze, okay? Even if you feel uncomfortable, try to relax and stay with my breathing."

I knew what was about to happen. I knew I was going to cry. It's not even about sadness—it's about vulnerability. Seeing into a person's soul, even for a moment, is just too much. It's like the convex meniscus Sylvia Plath describes in *The Bell Jar*—the water that clings to the sides of the glass before one tiny pulse causes it to overflow.

I followed Lauren's instructions and the tears flooded freely down my face, onto my chest. "Let them fall. It's good for you," she whispered and closed her eyes. "Jen, you have a guardian spirit with you here, someone who constantly protects you."

I sucked in air, waiting for this moment. "Is it my grandmother?"

"It's doesn't seem she's someone you knew—maybe an ancestor or other strong maternal spirit who's latched onto you. She's smiling. She's all love. She adores you. She adores how you adore others. You are a mother, aren't you?"

"I have one son," I said.

"Interesting, because I'm seeing a whole house full of children. Wait, no, a whole world. Are you a teacher?"

I grinned. This was the red flag I was waiting for—something about me that is easily researched. The skeptical side started creeping in, although, looking back, I can't recall giving my last name when I called for the appointment.

"Stay with me, Jen. There's someone else here. Someone who's passed over."

"Is it my grandma?" I ask again quickly.

"No, it's a man." The first person who came to my mind was my granddad, gone so many years now that I have to force myself to actively remember him for fear of him dissipating from my memory.

"A young man, Jen. Very young." My mind recalled far too many graduates that have died.

"Is it Keith?"

"No."

"Albert?"

"No."

"Victor?"

"No. This is a light-haired boy in a red sporty car. He's holding a bouquet out to you. Wait…" She quiets for a moment and her still face spread into a bright smile. "He says, 'Hey, beautiful.'"

The tears poured—tears of a young girl who was forced to say goodbye to her friend far too soon. "Of course. It's Paul."

"He's smiling, Jen."

The confusion turned to excavation, and in an instant, I was digging up that teenaged girl I'd tried so hard to bury. She was shallow. And weak. Blind to everything important. In a moment's breath I was swept back to West Chester, Pennsylvania, and my brain could not move quickly enough to keep up with the energy surging through me.

Paul, my freshman Biology lab partner, who cut through

the frog, so I didn't have to—laughing as I cringed at the tendons, the stomach, the lungs. "Here, Jen. I present to you my tiny heart." We both laughed at the globby frog part at the end of his scalpel.

Paul, at the bowling alley for his Make-a-Wish event. He donated the money to another child with Cystic Fibrosis because his own parents could afford to take him to Disney.

Paul, who raced to my house in his Honda Prelude as soon as he got his license—bursting in and fawning all over my mom. "You look scrumptious, Mrs. Weaver. Give me some sugar, Mrs. Weaver. Let's hold hands, Mrs. Weaver." My mother blushed, feigned disapproval, and hugged him like he was her own. Paul knew that mothers would never deny the sick kid.

Paul, my friend who drove me all over West Chester, blasting and singing every song on the radio—doing absolutely nothing except being young together.

Paul, who sat on the creek rocks in my back yard after a boy in our class died by suicide. "Here I am, just trying to hang on." He held me and apologized when I wouldn't stop crying.

Paul, who waited two years to ask me on a real date. When I said yes, my mother cried. "You can't fall for him, Jennifer. You know why, right?" I stormed to my room, blasted my stereo, drowning out reality.

Paul, who walked me to my doorstep one spring night and when he went to kiss my cheek, I held his face, looked into his eyes, and asked him if we should kiss—for real. His mouth pressed mine, and we stood on my front porch for what felt like hours, holding each other's hands, shoulders, necks, faces, breathing each other's breath, kissing like the world was going to end.

Paul, who understood when I became distant. Understood when I shied away. He didn't ask questions. He didn't become angry. He kissed my cheek and knew. His eyes showed only love. He didn't see me for the asshole I was.

Paul, who even still, asked me to prom, kissed my right collar bone to not mess up my prom makeup, played "Lady in Red" for me, and told me I was the most beautiful girl in class. We laughed knowing he said that to many girls. He yelled the word balls when the photographer said, "Say cheese," perfectly ruining my prom pictures.

Paul, who was almost crushed by a telephone pole in a drunk driving accident on graduation night. We held hands at Children's Hospital as he came to and flirted with my mom. His face was a mess, his leg was a mess, his pelvis was a mess, but we three laughed at his pretend advances until he we cried. "Stop. Stop. No crying. It's going to take more than a telephone pole crushing my balls to take me out of this world."

Paul, who wrote me letters in college. I still went away, but his recovery kept him at home.

Paul, who's health got progressively worse.

Paul, who called with an increasing rasp to his voice.

Paul, who held my hand when I was pregnant.

Paul, who held and kissed my baby.

Paul, who was on the transplant list

and got new lungs

and ran with the Olympic torch

and then sickness, waiting rooms, phone calls, rejection, organ failure.

Paul, who wouldn't say goodbye. Who preferred, "see you on the flip side."

And he was with me in that room. I could feel it.

Lauren opened her eyes and nodded. "He says he watches over you, Jen. He's in the car with you when you're driving, singing along. He keeps mentioning the passenger seat."

My mind returned to the space, to Lauren's hands, as she detailed more memories of our past. The night at Friendly's with the crazy waitress obsessed with napkins, Red Lobster cheddar biscuits, the red prom dress, the kiss on my collar bone, the Ocean City drunken after-prom party.

"Lauren, can you tell him that I'm sorry if I ever hurt him?"

She laughed. "He hears you. He's right here, and he's laughing that you would even say that. None of that matters after this world, Jen. We take the love with us. He knows how much you loved him and that you still do. It's really the only thing that lasts in this world and beyond it. But you already know that, don't you?"

I looked around the room as if I could catch a glimpse of him—a sign. All I wanted was to see a hint of his face and hear his voice restored to health. But all I saw was the smokey pink of the night sky.

My skin told a different story. Goosebumps raised and a warmth moved from my stomach to my throat. I sucked in the deepest inhale I've ever felt in my life.

"He's handing you the flowers, Jen. He's right inside your heart, and smiling."

Bloom

Tea brewed from sage has been used as a tonic for centuries, thought to promote wisdom, strength, and memory.

UNION CEMETERY

In memory of the unknown dead buried in this place.
Not even a sparrow falls to the ground
But what God
Knows...
Matthew 10: 29-30
—Cresson Union Cemetery, monument inscription

Union Cemetery sits at the top of the hill in Cresson, right off of Admiral Peary highway. It was founded in 1830, and in a town populated by mostly Catholics, was available to any Protestant needing a burial plot. Some older memorials have fallen over, others have sunk far below the grass level. The Cresson Cemetery Association has no records before 1950, and doesn't know where the records might be kept.

My grandmother hunched on the squat garden stool and snipped away at the grass. With the tiny plot's seedlings finally emerging, Grandma was intent on manicuring. It was an unseasonably hot day, and I was visiting for the Easter break. I helped her carry the water jugs from the car to the stoneless rectangle of land—they were the same gallon jugs we used to fill with spring water from St. Francis's shrine, but now, they were a bit weathered, and just for our cemetery trips.

Cresson Union Cemetery houses many of my family members—most of whom died well before I was born. It also serves as the final resting place for many people who resided at the Lawrence Flick Tuberculosis Sanitarium. There is a decent area of the grounds dedicated to these nameless individuals—people who were apparently forgotten in the throes of TB outbreaks from 1913 to 1960. Some of the graves have a faded name, others only a number. Every once in a while, a flower or two is left—a pop of color among the empty patch of land.

While Grandma landscaped Granddad's fairly fresh grave, I roamed the grounds. By the age of thirteen, I knew exactly where everyone was. Great-grandparents, great-great-grandparents, great-aunts and uncles. Even the baby. His little grave was the one I tended. There wasn't a traditional marker, only a tiny patch of flowers in the ground near his mother, Marian. There were complications during the delivery, and the baby died shortly after he was born; Marian passed a few days later. I suppose that's why they weren't buried together. If the baby had a name, we didn't know it, but we knew he was five steps north and ten steps west of Marian's grave. I had an intense fear that if I didn't keep the little flowers tended, the groundskeepers would try to bury someone else there, and it saddened me to think of his miniature coffin being disturbed after so many years of rest.

Marian's body has two markers: the headstone in Union Cemetery and the botched doorframe of my great-grandmother's house. In the spring of 1936, when my granddad and his brothers tried to fit their sister's coffin through the front door and into the parlor for the viewing, they discovered the casket was just too wide for the narrow passage. Grammy wanted her young daughter to be at home—shown in her own house—and she wasn't budging for another solution. She told her boys they were not to tilt the casket, so taking off the doorframe was the only answer. My great-grandfather told his wife she was crazy; they would think of another solution. Town legend has it, her response went something like this: She walked around the back of the house to the garden shed and returned with a sledgehammer. Wood splintered, plaster caved. Then, with the reverence of any queen's funeral, Marian's brothers and father carried her into the front parlor where Grammy set down the sledgehammer, opened the coffin, and then sat next to it, not moving, for two days. The door was haphazardly repaired. She kept its imperfections for as long as she remained in the house.

I sat my little gardening caddy next to the piece of land and knelt next to the grave that contained Marian's son—my third-cousin—gone for over fifty years. I plucked weeds, extracted the dead flowers, and broke apart the earth to plant some yellow pansies. The ground was dry, rare for this mountain town. I stabbed my spade through the dirt and added a little water. Such a tiny parcel of land situated between the other graves. We had tried to put a tree there for him, but the cemetery groundskeepers wouldn't think of it. "Too much to mow around already." This was also why Grandma couldn't get the stone she wanted for Granddad—it had to be flat for easier grounds maintenance.[3]

Grandma shouted down to me, "Did you take some Miracle Gro with you, Babydoll? Those flowers won't last long otherwise." She wiped her forehead with her sleeve and rubbed at her sore hands. She was working hard and had spent most of the winter itching to tend to the plot. We still had to wait awhile for the stone to go in, for the ground to settle.

Walking over my relatives' graves, I crossed the grounds where the forgotten TB patients were buried and paused. So many nameless; their only mark of existence, a number. My eyes burned and my throat tightened. I took a quick swig from my own St. Francis water jug as I made my way back up the hill to Grandma. "Here, baby." Grandma

---

3 Incidentally, this is why Grandma dug him up years later when she became very ill. I don't think she could stomach being buried in a cemetery that was only haphazardly taken care of, so they are buried in Alto-Rest, a perfectly manicured cemetery in Altoona, PA. Not my kind of resting place, but whatever. My still-very-much-alive parents have a stone there as well—a decision they did not run by me or Kim, and I suffered a lovely panic attack when I saw it and had to pop a Xanax.

On another note, with Granddad's old grave vacant, my cousins buried my Aunt Marilyn there.

scooped two mounds with her arthritic hands, and I cupped my palms to catch the soil. Her face was red, and her smile sincere. "You're a sweet little thing, you know that?" She squeezed my hands with hers and cocked her head. Grandma understood me. Later that night I would be with my friends—playing flashlight tag, buying treats at James' drugstore, looking through my sister's *Teen Magazines*—but at that moment, I was where I needed to be.

I walked the dirt back down the hill and folded it into the ground. The soil welcomed the pretty pansies as I covered their roots and watered them. A cool breeze raised my head, and Marian's grave caught my eye. Grandma said we would get to it another day, but it looked too sad to leave. Planting myself in front of her stone, I picked away at the weeds and dead flowers so that the word "Daughter" was visible at the bottom. Apparently, my great-grandfather was so distraught over her death, he wouldn't recognize her as a wife or a mother. She was his daughter, and if he was paying for the stone, that's how she would be remembered. Marian, as my grandma put it, "had to get married." She was pregnant, and my great-grandfather would not forgive Harry McGonigle for the indiscretion. I often wonder what he would say today if he knew that Harry McGonigle and his second wife visited Marian's grave on her birthday each year, placing pink tulips at the base of the stone. Would he find solace in Harry's devotion to his first love? Or would he still curse the man who corrupted his baby? I traced the word "daughter" with my finger thinking of Marian, of Grammy's doorframe, of the brothers carrying her casket, of leaving this world after only knowing its wonder for such a short time. Of the unknown.

Collecting my caddy, I dawdled back to Grandma. The sky was the most brilliant pink and orange that night. It was a sky of peace, renewal, and promise—the kind that reminds you of all things beautiful when life is not.

"Grandma, do you see this sky?" She was so hard at work that I thought she may have forgotten to look up. Grandma slowly lifted the water jugs.

"Well, look at that." She stood to rub her knees and limped to the trunk, placing the cracked water jugs inside. "I haven't seen a sky like that this early in the springtime in years. Did you finish planting your flowers? Want to get some ice cream?" I nodded and jumped in the front seat. Patsy Cline blaring on the radio, our hands still caked with dirt, we drove into the blazing pink sky that night—a springtime-summer drive that blanketed our silence like a thick balm.

CALM YOUR TITS

I stood in the small powder room, sweat dripping everywhere. What on earth could I use as a fan? I looked under the sink, grabbed a towel, and started swabbing off. Nothing about this was good. On the other side of the toilet I spotted a *Sports Illustrated* with a picture of Ben Roethlisberger on the cover. I stripped the dress off and awkwardly fanned my chest with Ben. Just outside the door, the chatter and laughter of high school seniors did nothing to abate my rising body temperature. The chicken cutlet-looking adhesive bra cups had seen better days.

Breasts tend to be a problematic mystery. I've always had to be mindful of these damn things, even in my earlier, flatter years. As a young girl, I envied the well-endowed, from the way they made a cream-colored cashmere sweater look to, sadly but honestly, the way they made boys stare.

They were like these magical mounds of power able to turn even the homeliest into demi-goddesses, casting spells through some kind of mammary-induced sorcery. Yes, I wanted them. I wanted that power. I wanted to buy sexy bras and have a fuchsia lace strap peek through the shoulder of my shirt. *Ha ha. Oops! Don't mind me as I fix all of my God-given sexiness right here in the middle of English class.* I just wanted to be pretty.

My teenage-boy body was not having it. I'd even look in the back of my mother's supermarket magazines and wondered if I could secretly mail in the money for the breast enhancing ads. It looked so easy, and the blond woman in the towel seemed incredibly confident and happy with her perfectly curved profile and Lonnie Anderson smile. I checked the mirror each morning and swore that I actually looked concave. I supposed God was cursing me for some youthful infraction. Didn't I once take five dollars from my mom's wallet? What about all those times I avoided playing with the smelly girl down the street? I knew my transgressions were catching up with me, and this was my punishment. I was destined to a life of flatness, loneliness, and perpetual cat-ladydom. But then, I grew up.

When I became a high school teacher, the prepubescent desire to actually possess these things turned into an issue of how to hide them. Each morning before work, my husband was put on breast patrol. At first he found it humorous, and a bit intriguing— smirking, oohing, ahhing. Then it just became an annoying morning ritual for us both, equivalent to taking the dogs out, getting Evan's backpack ready, and scrounging for lunch in an empty refrigerator. "Ryan, do you see a strap? Ryan, is this too low-cut? Ryan, can you see any hint of nipple through this shirt? Even a little bit?"

He would inspect, turn on the light, turn off the light, step back. "Jen, women have nipples. They just do. So do I, actually. Want to see them?" I'd defensively change my shirt into something a Puritan would wear and head out the door. And if it's cold, forget it. Find the thickest padded bra you can and pray to Saint Agatha, the patron saint of all breasts, that she would keep your yitties in check throughout the course of the frigid day.

The Great Bra Malfunction of 2003 could have driven anyone from the profession. There I was, teaching a twelfth grade remedial class of mostly seventeen- to eighteen-year old boys when *snap,* my bra completely gave. I ran from the classroom. They weren't the most observant children on the planet, but I knew if they were anything like my own husband, their radar for loose breasts would, at the very least, incite a ruckus enough to invoke Dionysus. Once safely in the English Department office, a veteran teacher recognized the familiar look of female panic, and with an arrangement of uncomfortable paper clips and staples, we sutured the torn fabric into what then resembled a medieval torture contraption—a steel fortress worthy of the androgynous look I momentarily craved. I was safe. My breasts, covered and forgotten. The boredom of the high school world could once again transpire.

It's why I was so insistent on the adhesive bra for Fran Rafferty's graduation party.

Having taught and loved all three Rafferty children, I became close to the family, and mourned the goodbye of the final child. The class of 2010, in general, was a favorite of mine. I typically head to the beach at the close of the school year, but upon receiving some sweet invitations to graduation parties, I felt compelled to attend. Fran's parents notified their guests that his party would have to be at a later time than initially planned because temperatures were supposed to spike well over 100 degrees. I rummaged through my coolest summer clothes, and while everything looked appropriate enough for the beach, nothing looked quite right for a high school party. I slipped into a chiffon spaghetti-strap, flowy dress. It was a little short and had a big V cut in the back, but it would have to do. "Does this look okay?"

Ryan examined, turned on the light, took a few steps back, and walked around me. "You know you can see your bra strap, right?" I spun around, craning my head to the mirror. Dammit. There, indeed was the pesky bra strap, significantly peeking from the bottom of the V. "Just don't wear one. It's not like you're going to be cold." I gasped at the suggestion, wondering if he had lost his mind. With a few minutes to spare, I ran to my drawer grabbing an adhesive bra that I had purchased on a whim—the miracle invention that was to, apparently, save the embarrassment of women everywhere. I paid close attention to the directions, alcohol-swabbed my chest to ensure it was free of natural oils and lotions, blew down on my boobs to guarantee they were dry, and smacked those babies on. They indeed looked like raw chicken cutlets—strange silicone-looking things that resembled some kind of alien life form. "Let me see, let me see," Ryan laughed through the door. There was no way in hell I was going to let him see. I slipped the flowy, A-line dress over my head and headed to the car.

The Raffertys were loved, very loved, as was evident by the lack of parking on their street. Looking back, I should have had Ryan drop me off at the driveway, but no, I decided to climb the street to his house. Gift in hand, we cut our way through the stifling humidity. Signal Hill Road indeed felt mountainous that evening. Making our way to the shaded backyard, the sweat started. First it was a small trickle down my neck, and then a waterfall through my cleavage. I shook hands, I hugged, and all the guests repeated the same exasperated sentiment, "Ugh. Sorry I'm so disgustingly sweaty." Everyone looked a mess, but surely, once in the shade with a cool drink, the sweating would stop.

It didn't.

The humidity was fierce, our drinks turned lukewarm in a matter of seconds, and the sweating wouldn't subside. "Ms. Rieger! Hey! So glad you could make it!" Fran's sister, Meghan, who had graduated the year before, ran to me, hugged me with all of the love in her little heart, and I felt it. The slipping of the right silicone cutlet. "Are you okay? Your face looks funny." I thought I was okay, at least okay enough to make it through a couple hours of the party.

"Of course, I'm okay!" I lied. "Maybe just a little sad to say goodbye to my Raffs." She hugged me again, walked away, and with that, the slippage got real. "Ryan," I whispered, "These adhesive boobs are slipping!" Ryan's eyes widened. I expected his face to mirror my own dread, but instead he started to laugh.

"I told you not to wear one." It's not what I wanted to hear, and I instantly wanted to kill him. As I stepped toward a nearby table to set down my drink and cup of ice, that's when it happened. The right cutlet slid, quickly, and I caught the damn thing in my crotch.

I find it so interesting, the events in my life when time actually seems to slow down—when an intruder entered our school, and I thought we were all done for, when I was six and got lost in the Empire State Building, when a dresser almost fell on Evan, and this, *The Great Tit Rebellion of 2010*. Coming back to a sense of time and place, I squeezed my thighs together as hard as I could.

"Ryan, I have to get to the bathroom. You walk behind me. If anything falls out of my crotch, grab it. Fast." Mr. Funny Guy suddenly looked as frightened as I was. I just needed to shuffle, a few steps at a time, carefully to the house, into the air conditioning, and surely I could fix this debacle. Thighs glued together, I cautiously skirted along the house, opened the side door, and a wave of even more oppressive air surrounded me. Janet Rafferty, Fran's mother, turned from her hot oven and greeted me with a hug.

"Jen! So great to see you!"

In true form of the day's misfortunes, the left cutlet started sliding. "Janet, I need a bathroom. I'm having an issue."

Janet's eyes widened in terror, "Oh God, please tell me it's not something you ate here."

I shifted my weight to adjust the crotch cutlet and assured her, "No, not that kind of problem." She pointed me around the corner and as I shuffled along, I was greeted by the other half of the entire senior class that wasn't in the yard. "Hey! Ms. Rieger!" Christ. I tried not to make eye contact. I couldn't hug another soul. I awkwardly entered the bathroom and locked the door.

I'm sure Janet thought my period was flowing down my legs. I'm sure my seniors thought I had explosive diarrhea. I would like to say I got to the point of not caring anymore, but I did. There I was, practically naked in the Rafferty's bathroom, soaking up a hand towel with cold water, trying to fix my breast fiasco. But the damage was done. The adhesive rebelled. I wrapped up the stupid culets as if they were a maxi pad, hid them at the bottom of the trashcan, fanned myself off as best as I could, and opened the door to enter the family room of children with my arms crossed over my chest.

And with that comedy of errors back in June of 2010, my boobs revolted. They were never the same again. They grew, one even slightly bigger than the other. My left one feels like it's on fire whenever I'm stressed out, and I'm pretty certain they're now in a conspiracy to thwart all bras. It was hubris. I went too far. My effort for prudence turned them into battling, mythical creatures that refuse to be controlled.

So, I had an epiphany. Instead of dealing with perpetual anxiety, after years of wanting these things, hating these things, worrying about friends and loved ones who have had numerous medical issues involving these things, I finally let it go, crossing out another item off my Bad Feminist List.

There was a time when I concerned myself with the rare slipped-expletive in front of students, hid my tattoos at all costs, and second-guessed myself about wearing jeans on a Monday. In addition to these small acts of rebellion, I'm adding *not giving a shit about my breasts anymore* to the list. The mere fact that I'm writing this is even a ridiculous risk I had to stress over, again causing my left boob to catch fire. Students will read it, parents will read it, administrators will read it, and maybe they will think, "Oh my God, she has breasts, and she's writing about them! The horror! The horror!" It speaks to something much bigger though—maybe we all need to calm the hell down. Maybe teachers can eventually live as normal human beings who have to pee during class, rip their bras and pants on occasion, stock tampons in their desk drawers, get lettuce stuck in their teeth, have sex, get pregnant, breastfeed, and goddammit, have visible nipples when it's fucking cold out. Maybe we can also one day have opinions and share them with the world without passive-aggressive, cowardly subtweets thrown into cyberspace. Maybe we can drink the wine at the local restaurant and hold hands with our partners, whether we fit a conventional societal standard or fall in love with, well, anyone. Maybe we can have a typo in a parent email, or better yet, call out shitty parents for not taking care of their kids. Maybe. Some day. One thing is clear, the year of my retirement, I'm going braless for the world to see. And if weekend family reunions are any indication of what these freed babies will look like, it's going to be a spectacle. Let's face it, if I hate bras this much in my 40s, I'm going to be one salty bitch about them in my 60s. The entire school district will be disgusted by my lack of discretion, and I will revel in my ornery, old lady sass. I will meet my best friends for a glass of wine at Peppers, toast St. Agatha, toast being teachers and strong women, toast the kids we've adored and have taken care of for decades, and post a picture on social media for all the world to see, and judge.

BECOMING JEN

In the fall of 1994, I was a new mom, a new wife, and a faithful fan of the brand-new sitcom, *Friends*. I looked forward to Thursday night TV all week. I had just turned twenty-one, and after a full day of changing diapers, watching *Barney*, and reading Shakespeare, I would glue myself to my grandma's hand-me-down console TV in our first apartment and pretend I was carefree again. I imagined myself, along with my own friends, living it up in Manhattan, drinking from oversized coffee cups, and popping in and out of each other's apartments. I imagined being thin again, wearing cute clothes, and sitting next to my husband on the couch in Central Perk as we all contributed to the most trivial and inane conversations. I imagined being Rachel.

Rachel Green was incredibly cute and fairly flawed. She almost let societal expectations undermine her self-worth and forge a path which, for her, meant complacency. But she didn't. She didn't go through with a loveless marriage, and she decided instead to make it on her own. She cut up Daddy's credit cards and went from barista to fashion buyer. With her adorable new haircut that took Gen X-ers by storm, Rachel became somewhat of an icon to young women. This isn't to say she was a perfect role model. Her spoiled upbringing, episodic bouts of whining, and at times, air-headed nature could set anyone on edge. But she was also kind of real—a young woman questioning privilege, battling her own inflated ego, seeking a way to remain true to herself and true to her friends. Watching her was a fun escape and actually made me contemplate the person I did and did not want to be. Learning about Jennifer Aniston over the years, or Jen as I like to call her, was even more interesting. Her attitude toward aging, beauty, charity, heartbreak, and motherhood left me in awe. It became clear that it wasn't Rachel I admired; it was Jen.

Jennifer Aniston wrote an article for *The Huffington Post* voicing her frustration over incessant pregnancy rumors. She states, "For the record, I am *not* pregnant. What I am is *fed up*." At the time of the article, Jen was forty-seven. You would think there would be a point when people stop prodding her, when they start minding their own business. I know too well they won't. I imagine when Jen is sixty-five and I am sixty, when our eggs have long since dried up, our friends, families, and co-workers (a.k.a. Mr. and Mrs. Well-Meaning) will ask, "So, when are you having a baby?" Her experience is different than mine, obviously. First of all, she's a celebrity and is under the microscope every day; additionally, she has never had a baby. On the other hand, I've had one child and, on many occasions, have been made to feel like a neglectful parent because of my son's only-child-existence. What unites us is that we are both apparently unnatural—both freaks in a world that loves labels, and traditions, and tiny patriarchal boxes.

Once upon a time, there was another Jen. I went to middle school and high school with Jen Wylie—my goofy, lovely choir friend. Jen and I didn't often socialize outside of school. She did have one crazy party sophomore year that our classmates still talk about to this day. It looked like a scene right out of *Sixteen Candles*. Beer covered her parents' floors, tables ended up broken, beds were, good God, besmirched. So when she got pregnant shortly after graduating from high school, we were all quite surprised; it was still assumed she was grounded for the rest of her natural life.

Her baby girl was beautiful—the perfect combination of Jen's sweet face and the face of her husband, Roman, the older football god we all had a crush on growing up. She seemed happy. It was all working out. And she conveyed this to me with a phone call after hearing that I was pregnant. Baby gurgles in the background, I sat on my kitchen floor, tracing the patterns in the tiles with my fingers, listening to Jen explain everything I was about to encounter and asking me questions I had only recently pondered. Was I taking prenatal vitamins? Did I see the doctor yet? Did I hear the heartbeat? Some questions took me to the world of adulthood that I still couldn't face. Would I need WIC or medical assistance? Bottle or breastfeed? Natural childbirth or epidural anesthesia? My mind was in a whirl. Wasn't it just yesterday that I listened to New Kids on the Block with this girl? Wasn't it just yesterday that I borrowed her lip gloss in choir?

Shortly after I had my baby, Jen had another. And then another. And then eight more. And then three grandbabies. She exudes a magical, maternal force that is, quite honestly, enviable. Her Facebook posts scream of her art—nurturing her gorgeous family. It is a gift I don't possess, and I've been well aware of that for a very long time.

Mr. and Mrs. Well-Meaning have stalked Jen's life too, only with different questions: How do you feed them? Are they all from the same marriage? How much does your husband make? Because, you see, this other Jen is a freak too. Just like me. Just like Jennifer Aniston.

But here is what Mr. and Mrs. Well-Meaning, with all of their questions and concerns, don't know: They don't know our lives. They don't know which Jen lies awake at night scared about decisions of the past, scared about screwing up the present—scared about regret in the future. They don't know which Jen prays to one day cradle her first tiny person, or yet another tiny person, of her very own. They don't know which Jen lives in certainty, confident and proud of her life choices. They don't know which Jen is infertile, and is in turn, stung by feelings of inadequacy and hopelessness every time there's a comment. They don't know which Jen's ovaries burn every time she holds a baby or if each day crossed off the calendar is another reminder of a window that inches closed, just a little bit more. They don't know which Jen has suffered painful loss, and therefore, holds a much different appreciation of new life. The "concerned men" don't know what carrying a baby for nine months does to a person. How a little piece of your heart is taken from you, leaving you a helpless bystander to a part beautiful, part cruel world that you hope will be kind and fair, but you know is certain to incite pain. They don't know which Jen swallows down the pangs of envy whenever her friends send beautiful holiday cards of fresh, toothless smiles. They don't know which Jen rejoices each day, or which Jen cries each night. And, most of all, Mr. and Mrs. Well-Meaning, with all their vague, but let's face it, snarky and intrusive intentions, obviously don't know how to shut their mouths.

The funny thing about this life is, it's supposed to be our own. We're supposed to be able to decide what's best for us, pay our bills, and be kind to people without bowing to societal expectations, whether that includes having eleven kids or none. When I see Jennifer Aniston in commercials and new movies, exuding confidence with her Aveeno-kissed skin, I feel like a proud little sister. I know it sounds ridiculous; she doesn't even know I exist. But I like to imagine that when she holds the children at St. Jude Hospital, speaks passionately about her work with orphans in Tijuana, and advocates for LGTB youth, her heart matches my own. Maybe she feels the same way I feel when my only child shares good news with me, when I sense that he's hurting, when my students come to me with problems, and when they return to me well after they graduate. Maybe she feels like my high school friend Jen when her oldest daughter walks in the door holding her grandbaby or when her youngest cuts his first tooth.

See, I know a little secret that Mr. and Mrs. Well-Meaning fail to recognize: maternal love has little to do with what they've been told or the expectations of family and friends. It reaches far beyond the baby-bumps, 2.5 kids, and white-picket fences. Their well-meaning questions only serve as a glaring spotlight into their own lives, into their own insecurities.

SUPERTRAMPS

Rather than love, than money, than fame, give me truth.
— Henry David Thoreau

Every year, when my students study the writings of Byron, Thoreau, and Sharon Olds, I show the movie *Into the Wild*, and we read passages from the book by Jon Krakauer. In short, it's the true story of Chris McCandless, a recent Emory graduate, who takes on the name Alexander Supertramp, deciding to shed his earthly possessions, donate his trust fund to charity, and venture across the country to find meaning and solace in the Alaskan wilderness. Alone. I always have students, typically boys, who develop a mild obsession with McCandless' experience. They read Krakauer's complete text, buy the movie for themselves, delve into McCandless' favorite authors, and then they go back to their high school world of sports, social media, and video games.

But Jamie was different.

I had known Jamie from the time he was a little elementary school tyke. Evan was friends with his younger brother, and the three played little league baseball together. On his first day in my class, as I reviewed the year's expectations and curriculum, his eyes lit up. "During our exploration of self-reliance and journey, we'll watch some clips from the movie *Into the Wild*." Little did I know, Jamie had already watched the movie approximately fifty times, memorized the Eddie Vedder soundtrack, and read the complete works of Thoreau. He also inspired his group of friends to do the same. Pat, Connor, and Moe—they were all infatuated. We had a blast with the unit. They made it special for everyone, and Jamie even tattooed his arm with the famous Thoreau quote.

One day Jamie said, "Ms. Rieger, you know I'm following his journey someday, right? Not anytime soon, but someday."

Did I worry? A little.

With the magic of social media, I get to maintain a distant, but lovely connection to many of my graduates. The beauty is, they still feel like mine. The tragedy is, they still feel like mine. I applaud their achievements from afar and worry when I sense danger.

Jamie successfully made his way through an unconventional college experience at Prescott College in Arizona. He climbed mountains as he read poetry and zip-lined through trees while studying environmental science.

After graduating, he showed up in my classroom at the end of the school day, unexpectedly of course. "Ms. Rieger. I'm doing it. I'm going to travel the coast a bit, but then I'm doing it. Alaska. I just had to say thank you and goodbye." Without even asking, I knew he was embarking on this alone.

"Jamie. Honey. What are you hoping to find?" I wasn't trying to make him stay—it would have been a fruitless endeavor anyway. Maybe I wanted to know for myself.

"I don't know, Riegs. What are any of us looking for? Whatever that unknown is, that's what I'm hoping to find." His bear hug lifted me off of the floor. It was the same hug I remembered from graduation night at Villanova Pavillion except that particular hug was followed with words I'll never forget: "Ms. Rieger, there's more out there than this little microcosm. Your heart is too big for this place." And with the air of a wise, old sage, diploma in hand, he walked away.

It was autumn. Brittle leaves fell in annual promise, and the newness of the year had subsided into a comfortable warmth of senior activity. Given that I only had a short time left with my students before my approaching sabbatical, I was embracing every second with them. We had just finished an insightful discussion of *Our Town*, and I was making my way "into the wild." It was exciting. I knew they would love it.

We began the unit with an analysis of Lord Byron's "Childe Harold's Pilgrimage." Students came into class with scribbled marginalia of figurative language examples and analyses on form, tone, and meaning. "Give me your thoughts on, 'I love not man the less, but nature more.'" I prodded, making my way around the room, calling out the quiet ones who tried to avert their eyes. Sasha looked contemplative. She was always the first one with her hand up—one of those kids I can count on to save a sinking lesson. Today, her gears were turning. She needed time to process, but finally spoke up. "There's a power to nature; it's fierce, consuming. Dangerous. The speaker finds answers there. This doesn't take away his love of man, because man is a part of that very beauty. That love is also fierce, also consuming, but maybe lacks the same kind of relief." Desk slap.[4]

We watched *Into the Wild*; we made connections. We discussed smallness and bigness, safety and the unknown, naiveté and calculated risk. They were a group of seventeen- and eighteen-year-olds blowing my mind. Some felt McCandless was selfish and foolish, leaving behind those he loved for a sense of personal glory and then, dying a lonely death inevitably hurting those he left behind. Their words had been echoed among these cinderblocks before, but I always get the Jamies of the world ready to defend some kind of secret explorer code. This year, it was my Supertramp Kids.

Upon watching the film, Sasha and her best friends,

4 I'm known for slapping the desk, hard, any time my kids are particularly brilliant. I once broke a lovely bracelet this way. Tiny, colorful beads flew everywhere.

Jessie, Shelby, and Sarah, developed a fascination with the book and the ancillary readings that accompany it. McCandless's spirit spoke to them. They knew there was more out there. They wanted to immerse themselves in nature and beauty. They wanted to feel in control of their own personal freedom. Each weekend I received a new picture from them—sneakers and boots next to a lonely creek, the book itself with all of their hands on it, their own creative Supertramp names inscribed into a snowy field. They were inspired. They were doing it. Embracing small journeys, they took the opportunity to discuss language, and meaning, and life. The spark they generated was far greater than any physical journey. Yes, they were in the safety of our community. Yes, they returned to the warmth of their parents' homes each night. Those far-off destinations will be there for them, some day. For now, they desired deliberate engagement into learning, finding themselves—finding each other.

Jamie went on his Alaskan adventure, and I followed his Instagram intently, waiting for updates on his progress. Sporadically, pictures emerged from distant places and unfamiliar explorations: shooting Japanese sake in Lake Tahoe, hiking mountains in Vail, and wading in crystal waters. Then finally, there were pictures of the preparation— the backpack, the sleeping bag, the camping gear. He was finally doing it. Going off the grid was something he always wanted. I waited for a new picture, holding my breath.

At the same time Jamie was on his great Alaskan

adventure, I was vacillating between life choices. My MFA thesis was fast approaching, and I wanted it to be good. It would be my first book, after all. My dreams of a becoming a writer finally coming to fruition. I'd had a rough time the year prior, and although I never doubted being a teacher, after twenty years, I was wondering if I needed some distance. I put in the paperwork for a Professional Compensated Leave, and it was approved. Jamie returned, regaling me with his stories, and his signature smile stretched across his face when I told him about my own decision.

I've never known an adult life outside of this school, but once upon a time, I thought I was destined for other things. The ghost ship I assumed had drifted years ago, had reappeared. I registered for a writing workshop in Sicily in January and charted my own journey along the Pacific coast: Seattle, Portland, the redwoods, Sonoma, San Francisco, with the sounds of plane engines, train tracks, car radios, and babbling brooks as my muses. My goals were deliberate: to write my ass off; force myself to meet new people and learn from them; be young in spirit and aged in appreciation; come back home knowing what I want in this life. When I returned, Jonathan, my principal listened to my stories and applauded my discoveries. "All those places, all of those beautiful landscapes. They must have been magical, Jen."

I paused for a moment and stared into the hallway. It was in between bells and students were running to their next classes, laughing with their friends. "No more magical than my dirty, old classroom upstairs." And it was true. How loving those excursions and loving my students could be so equally rewarding is one of the greatest lessons I'll ever bear witness to. I know many writers who teach, and they're good at both. Once upon a time I wanted to be one of them. But after all of the drama early in my career, I know without any measure of doubt, I am a teacher who just happens to occasionally write. They come first because that school is my home; those kids are my home. It was scary leaving them in the hands of a complete stranger, knowing that someone else heard about their college acceptances— someone else got to experience all their "lasts." I had to break my own heart, and while that was torture, the truth is, they're still my kids. My limited time with them brought us even closer. We knew the reality of our short window, so we held on, learned from each other even more. My Supertramps. Even when they're not with me, they're cheering for me, inspiring me, telling me to push boundaries of expectation. This life is turning out to be shorter than I anticipated; the years fly with such a lovely and frightening ease. I think I'll hold on, tighter.

EVERYDAY SACRED

It was early September, and Anna Derby and I decided to meet at Starbucks. I marveled at how the summer had escaped me. It had already been three months since her Valedictorian speech, three months since her sweet letter to me, three months since we said goodbye. I missed her—this nervous, over-achieving Jesus lover.

I had taught Anna's brother two years prior, and I adored Mitch. So funny, so smart. He was a complete goofball with his friends, but he'd do anything in the world for me. Anna possessed the same kindness as her brother but, as with most siblings I teach, there were some striking differences. Anna worried. About everything. She worried about my class, about maintaining her flawless academic record, and about the next step in life. She was also devoutly religious.

Our community is a mixed bag of cultures and faiths. It's

one of the reasons I love it and why I wanted my son to grow and learn here. He was exposed to roughly everything— Christians, Jews, Muslims, Hindus, Buddhists, Pagans, agnostics, atheists, new-age-hippie-humanists—and I'm sure I'm missing something. All have taught me important lessons; all have enriched my view of the world. For almost twenty years now, I have been given the opportunity to wander out of my little Judeo-Christian bubble and explore, question, doubt. It was awkward as hell at first. I am, after all, a public school teacher, and a full believer of the separation of church and state. But I also made sense of that for myself. "Separation" doesn't have to mean ignoring an important part of a student's life. Similar to political discussion, eating in class when you're hungry, and wearing denim when I damn well please, the taboo of religion in the classroom now falls under my veteran-teacher category of "Things I Do Not Give a Shit About Anymore." If it adds to our class discussion or enhances a piece of writing, go for it. When students write about God in their college essays, I take the opportunity to question a little more about their faith and culture—how they grew up, what kind of role this plays in their lives, will it be a deciding factor in their choice of college. Sounds pretty idyllic, right? Such a sweet little suburban melting pot. Nothing is ever that easy.

A romantic to the core, I want to be a believer. I want to be among the faithful. But just when I think I have a solid handle on spirituality, when I'm one with the universe, I'm slapped in the face with ugliness—childhood cancer, hunger, refugees, mental illness. Additionally, take a look at the history of religion, or even open a newspaper. Hypocrisy is everywhere.

But Anna was different, and she brought a new perspective to my classroom. She was high on Jesus, and it was genuine. She didn't focus on church "rules," political ridiculousness, or try to convince others that they should believe what she believed. She possessed a pure devotion to the teachings of Christ—goodness, love, compassion, selflessness, honesty, generosity. And even though she was incredibly hard on herself at times, she turned to her faith for guidance and reassurance and, what a love, sometimes she turned to me.

There are a few people in my life whose hearts are so rare, they don't deserve to live in a world this cruel. Their presence heals. Their energy restores. Their love is so intense that it leaves me feeling so very big and so very small all at the same time: a fellow teacher whose quiet but strong belief in progress turned into the battle cry of our school's character education movement; two former students whose love of learning transcends this world; a college professor who helped me to use my words, find my voice and to rise up in the shadow of stigma and self-doubt; two poet friends who have the ability to reach into my soul with their verse, and into my heart with their eyes. And Anna is one of these people.

We spent a year discussing literature, writing, college, friendship, and love. I listened intently as she merged her faith into every aspect of her life, beautifully molding her world. While there were many days when she sat chatting away in my blue chair, our deepest conversation was through e-mail. Classic twenty-first century emotional connection. She had sent me a spoken word poem by a Christian poet she liked, and we went back and forth discussing its meaning and how it related to our lives.

I'm not a church goer. The irony is, I love churches—especially old ones. I like to research their history, wander their cemeteries. If they have crypts, damn, even better! I like to sit in sanctuaries by myself and think, not even necessarily about faith, but about anything. Sometimes I like to take my journal into a quiet corner and write, allowing the light piercing its way through the stained glass to dance across my lifeless paper, across my aging skin. The faces of the saints cheer me on, smiling down on the particularly bad days. Sometimes the smell of old wood, books, and dissipated incense calms me in a way no glass of wine can. Sometimes I lower the kneelers, perch myself quietly, and stare at the ceiling in wonder knowing that after centuries upon centuries of scientific study, doubt, plague, and war, sacred mystery remains. And it will. After I'm gone. After you're gone. Until the day when mothers stop gazing into their babies' faces in awe, the day all of the addicts hitting bottom give up, the day artists put down their pens and brushes, the day society stops fearing death, faith will permeate through the walls of collective memory and linger in the corners of our DNA.

In all her perfectionist glory, Anna became one of the class's eight valedictorians. She almost self-sabotaged by purposely getting a B to avoid speaking at graduation. I gently scolded her, reminding her to stay true to herself, that she didn't have to speak if she didn't want to. But the more I met with my amazing dream team of academics—crafting, editing, rehearsing—the more excited Anna became to face her public speaking fear and stand with her peers. It was a beautiful speech that encapsulated all eight personalities. They worked diligently, in person and online. As graduation night approached, Anna said to me, "Do you know where you'll be sitting? I'm so nervous, but I think if I just look at you I'll be okay." We made a plan, and on the big night, that's exactly what she did. She delivered her part with the grace she's known for, not taking her eyes off of me as I mouthed the words along with her. When it ended, she glowed, and that light I feel from her whenever she's around permeated the entire pavilion—the love of her class, her family, her teachers. Her love of God.

We hugged after graduation at the Villanova Pavilion, and my thoughts soared back to one of our final heart-to-hearts. "Ms. Rieger. I wish you would come to my church with me sometime." Through all of my conversations with students, it was the only time one had invited me.

"Anna, you are such a blessing, and thank you. But that's not for me. My church is my classroom. It's my interactions with friends in coffee shops. It's my mom's dinner table on Christmas night. It's the hospital room when my students are sick, injured, or dying. It's the school auditorium on Ivy Day. It's Challenge Day. It us here and now. Does that make sense to you?"

I knew it did, before she even said it. Inviting me was simply her way of sharing something she loved most in her life with a person she loved. And I was honored. Anna was discerning enough to know I struggled with religion, with extremists, with hypocrisy, and even though I was raised a Christian and had a positive experience with the United

Methodist Church, the adult "organized" part of church left me unsettled. I still go from time to time when life gets hard, when I need to hear sacred music or words of comfort, or when I want to be reminded of the tiny church in Cresson where I spent my summers. Am I the hypocrite? Maybe. I place offerings in the church collection plate for my gratitude and guilt, and I leave. Maybe I'll return in a few months, maybe in a few years. Or maybe I won't. Maybe I'll just be content to embrace the everyday blessings of my life.

YOU MEAN TED HUGHES'S WIFE?

There is a certain unique and strange delight about walking down an empty street alone. There is an off-focus light cast by the moon... You get a feeling of being listened to, so you talk aloud, softly, to see how it sounds.
— *The Unabridged Journals of Sylvia Plath*

"You know, she was quite crazy, that one. Don't go sticking your head in an oven after you read it." As a naïve senior in high school, I had no clue what my English teacher, Dr. Powers, meant, so I took her warning with a smile and only a slight eye roll. I had to select a text for our independent novel study, and I was incredibly bored by Dr. Power's fascination with Victorian authors. In part curiosity and part spite, I chose and devoured Sylvia Plath's *The Bell Jar*. When it ended, I went back to page one and started over, looking closer at nuance, figurative language, and subtle wit.

I wanted more. I knew the novel was semi-autobiographical, so I headed to the library to conduct some research. And I learned—not only about her life, but also about her death. I also learned Dr. Power's joke wasn't very funny. Plath was brilliant, no doubt, and I knew people were often put off by her because she was, *"Oh God, soooo depressing!"* Right. And all of the other great works of literature are so uplifting? I wasn't a closet depressive, had never been suicidal, but there was something about the plight of the protagonist, Esther Greenwood, that took hold. Even though the novel was set in the 1950s, everything was relatable—drinking, sex, self-doubt, pregnancy, motherhood—it spoke to me. I too felt at times like the eye of a tornado watching the hullabaloo of the world circle around me. I too felt like the girl sitting in the crotch of the fig tree watching life's choices ripen and fall if not picked quickly enough.

After a long day in London with my study abroad group, I decided to spend the night in Primrose Hill where Sylvia lived in two residences—one with her acclaimed poet laureate-husband, Ted Hughes, and then one on her own with their two children. Hannah, my hostess at Primrose House, showed me to my room at the top of the inn. My day of incessant walking was intense, and I longed for the clean bed and shower, but instead of making myself at home, I thanked her, changed into some jeans and a sweatshirt to face the August chill of Primrose Hill. It was a sweet little borough—flowers everywhere—and I quickly snapped a selfie in front of a red phone booth. The Starbucks on the corner looked invitingly like home, and I had been craving my definition of "real coffee" all week, even though half and half doesn't exist in England. I also had little idea where I was going save for a sketchy map I screenshotted on my phone. I placed the order for my grande coffee and mustered the courage to ask for directions to the house of a dead woman.

"Excuse me. I was wondering if you could help me." I began hesitantly. "I'm looking for the former house of the late Sylvia Plath. I know it's in this neighborhood. Is this map any good?"

The poor girl looked like she wanted to cringe at my Philly accent and obviously had little idea what I was talking about. "She was a poet who died in 1963."

"Richard!" she yelled. "Please come out here. There's a question I'm sure I have no answer to."

Richard appeared looking annoyed. He was maybe all of two days older than my confused barista. Richard's brow furrowed in response to my question, so he in turn yelled across the shop, "Hello, Burt! Could you come over here for a moment? This lady has a question about some poet."

"Ahh… Would it happen to be Keats?" An old man of about eighty hobbled toward me with an excited look on his face. "I can take you there m'self if you'd like." I could tell immediately this old man was a charmer. His outfit of khakis, crisp white button down, and light sport coat with elbow pads spoke volumes. He wasn't at one of the nicer restaurants in town; he was at Starbucks, but he looked like the mayor.

"I'm so sorry to bother you, and no, I'm not looking for

Keats at the moment. I'm looking for the home of Sylvia Plath." Burt paused, looking just a tad deflated. I think he was dying to discuss Keats, which I was too, only the sun was setting. Even though it was becoming increasingly apparent that my chances of getting murdered in Primrose Hill were slim, I still had little business walking around London by myself late at night. Plus, the newspaper headlines that very morning were seared into my brain. AMERICAN WOMAN STABBED TO DEATH IN LONDON. My mother had already been texting me every nightmare she could possibly conjure, to which I kindly reminded her that I live in Philadelphia.

"Hmm." Burt took a moment to stare at the floor. "Do you happen to mean Ted Hughes's wife?" Was this guy serious? Instantly, my blood started boiling, and I readied myself to defend the honor of my dead poet I had studied for so long. My interest in Sylvia's writing didn't end in high school. As an undergrad, I concentrated my English studies in women's literature and then became fairly serious in studying Plath's poetry throughout my master's coursework and thesis. For such an adorable young woman, Sylvia was a rather dark and twisty poet, and I liked that. She was willing to explore life through a murky window that most people would rather keep tightly shut. Granted, she dwelled there quite regularly, but her examination of endings, death, and loss opened a world to the ephemeral nature of things. I've been known to enjoy strolling through the occasional cemetery and ancient crypt. I have also been known to mourn the passing of time; but it has only made me embrace the incredible individuals in my life even more.

It's also taught me gratitude. In her personal life, Sylvia had a difficult time finding this, and an even more difficult time holding onto it. Her marriage to Ted Hughes did not end well. After dealing with years of his infidelity, the couple separated. Their divorce hadn't been finalized when she died, and Hughes took some creative liberties with her final collection of poems, *Ariel*, and even went as far as to burn her last journal. Needless to say, his choices did not make him a sympathetic figure to Plath followers. Dead two decades, he's still not.

Calmly remembering that I was a guest in Ted Hughes's country, I took a deep breath and answered the sweet old man. "Yes, that's the one. Sylvia Plath Hughes. I'm looking for the house they lived in when they were married and then the one she died in. The latter was also inhabited by William Butler Yeats for a time. Does that help any?" I showed him the map on my phone, and he confirmed some of the smaller road directions that confused me. Burt had kind, youthful eyes that didn't match his wise, weathered face; I liked him. He was the classic grandfather out of every storybook, and brilliant. We talked for a bit about my travels, the thesis I wrote for my first master's, and the Sylvia journey I was currently undertaking. "Burt, could we meet for a pint or a glass of wine after I find her houses? I'd love to pick your brain a bit about Keats."

"Oh, no, no. Your husband might not like you associating with such a handsome English scoundrel on your solo journey across the pond." He and Richard exchanged glances, and they both laughed. "Besides, I stopped drinking when my wife died. It makes me all warm, red, and weepy."

Yes. It did do that.

"It makes me all warm, red, and weepy too; but, it also invokes my writing muse." Burt patted my hand and kissed it. I grabbed my coffee, and he escorted me from Starbucks. "Now remember, up the hill and then down. Good luck finding your dead American poet." With a quick hug, we parted ways. The sun was setting.

I turned and curved my way through Primrose Hill, finding the house where she and Ted lived on Chalcot Square where her official London blue plaque[5] resides, and then, finally, finding the one I was really looking for—the house on Fitzroy Road, where she died. Sylvia liked that Yeats once lived there; she took it to be a "good omen." It's a lovely green, white, and brick, three-story house that has been well maintained and graces the Yeat's blue plaque to the right of the door. The top floor looked empty, but the ground floor had lights on and the shadows of its residents suggested life.

I stood there, not certain what I was supposed to feel. I snapped some pictures and stared for a few more minutes. I can recall years ago being mortified that Sylvia didn't have a blue plaque there as well, but I think it makes sense to me now. She was so young. The winter of 1963 had been one of the coldest in London history, and Sylvia was alone in

---

5 From the Blue Plaque page of the *English Heritage* website (http://www. english-heritage.org.uk/):

"London's famous blue plaques link the people of the past with the buildings of the present. Now run by English Heritage, the London blue plaques scheme was started in 1866 and is thought to be the oldest of its kind in the world. Across the capital over 900 plaques, on buildings humble and grand, honour the notable men and women who have lived or worked in them."

that top flat, sick with a toddler and an infant. She couldn't get the medication for her depression right, tried reaching out to friends for help, but inevitably could not lift the descending bell jar that seemed to hover about her all her life.

The orangey-pinks of the sky beckoned me onward, and I made my way over to an outdoor café a few properties down. I quietly toasted her last home and downed the perfect glass of Pinot Noir before groggily climbing Primrose Hill again. The next leg of my journey was going to be long, and I was tired.

"I think you have a strong proposal here, Jen. The idea of Plath's 'separate self' reflecting the confessional literary tradition is compelling. You've done a lot of work on her already. Yes, honey. I'd be happy to be your thesis adviser." Anne Kaier smiled at me, her aged hand patting my own. I loved this woman. Interestingly enough, she looked a bit like Dr. Powers, but she had the heart of a mother bear and watched over her graduate students as if we were her very own. She was proud of me too, constantly asking about Ryan and Evan and even remembering the names of my students we discussed. All of this, and she was absolutely brilliant.

I was excited to begin the thesis—excited to peel back the surface of Plath's verse and dig inside of her. What makes the collection more of "Ariel" and less of "Daddy?" Why the tulips? I had so many questions—ones that would take me to Smith College archives maybe, or even her hometown in Massachusetts. I knew that although *The Bell Jar* was near the end for her, it was only the beginning for me. I knew my answers would lie in her poetry.

After a day of travelling by foot, car, bus, and multiple trains from King's Cross Station in London, I stood at the train depot in Hebden Bridge, West Yorkshire, completely lost. It was the first hot day since I had arrived in England, of course, and I looked like an absolute wreck. The sun blazed, and I needed to find my inn before my duffle bag broke my shoulder. I knew I shouldn't have brought so many research materials, but it was either that or have an exorbitant bill of racked up data charges. Everything was sticking to me. I needed to get settled. I needed to locate a local map. I needed to find Sylvia.

Hebden Bridge is an idyllic town. Once known for its wool and weaving industry, it's now home to artists, musicians, and writers. I felt a bit disjointed—being pulled back to a medieval village and a 1960s hippie commune at the same time. I questioned the first person I found about the location of my inn—a teenage boy I almost ran right into.

"Oh, sure, I can help," he said. "Lived here all m'life. Just keep following this road up the hill, and the White Lion Inn will be on your right."

I thanked him, and walked. And walked. And walked. With books. I flipped on my cellular data and opened Google Maps. The little shit sent me in the wrong direction. I turned around.

The White Lion Inn is an absolutely gorgeous historic public house covered in English ivy and blooming flowers. The only entrance is through the restaurant, and I knew I looked a fright as I approached the bar.

"Morning, ma'am. I can check you in here." A cute young girl greeted me and flashed the most perfect smile. Probably sensing that I was about to fall over, she poured me a glass of water as I relayed my information. "Yes, Ms. Rieger. You're booked with us for one night, but I'm sorry, your room will not be ready until 3:00. Can we store your bag while you explore the town?" I gladly gave her my heavy duffel and inquired about the best way to get to St. Thomas' Cemetery. "Not sure if I know of it. Mark!" The girl yelled to the back of the pub, and I felt an overwhelming sense of déjà vu.

Mark appeared, an equally attractive individual. Both of them only accentuated the grossness that I was currently permeating. I asked Mark the same question and showed him the screen shot of the Heptonstall map. "Please tell me I'm in the right place. It's been a long journey. I'm looking for Sylvia Plath's grave."

"Oh! Ted Hughes's wife!"

Dear Lord.

Mark squinted at the screen and put on his glasses. "Ah. You're looking for Heptonstall Village. You're in Hebden Bridge. Looks like the church is two miles away."

"Perfect," I said. "Is there any place I can rent a bike?" The waitress and Mark looked at each other, trying to stifle a laugh.

"Are you a cyclist, ma'am?" Mark looked at me with

all sincerity, but I had my back up. Was this guy mocking me with his youthful glow and sparkling smile? I was not in the mood for humor or additional smartasses on this trip. "I beg your pardon, ma'am. It's two miles on a straight incline," Mark kindly added.

Well, shit.

Incline was a bit of an understatement, and I was ill-prepared for a hiking expedition. Donning ripped jeans, Toms shoes, and wearing the worst possible bra for sweating, I quickly braided my hair into two makeshift pigtails. I weighed the option of spending some time in town to find workout clothes and hiking shoes, but I quickly dismissed the idea and carried on. How bad could it be?

Everyone I encountered along the way looked at me with the same grin Mark and the waitress had. One kind old man stopped me and asked if I was alright. "Oh, yes. Just hot." I stopped to feel the cool breezes at the guardrail's edge, trying not to become roadkill by the occasional speeding car.

He rummaged through his bag, took out a small bottle of water, and handed it to me. "Shouldn't climb Heptonstall Hill without water, young lady."

I drained the bottle, thanking him profusely. "I believe I started this journey by leaving my common sense back in Philadelphia."

The old man smiled. "Well, sometimes common sense holds us back, now, doesn't it? What exactly are you trying to find?" He handed me a folded handkerchief from his bag.

It was a good question. A very good question. Wanting to say *I have no idea*, I managed, "I'm looking for the grave of Sylvia Plath," and I quickly added, "Ted Hughes's wife." I wiped my brow and neck, staring at the road.

"Ahh! I hear she was quite a good poet. Sad, sad ending to her life. You know, Hughes's parents lived in Heptonstall." Yes, I had known that. When staying with Ted's parents, Sylvia wrote the poem "November Graveyard" based on the very cemetery she is ironically buried in.

"Thank you for your help. Seriously. Would you like your now sweaty handkerchief back?" We both laughed.

"No, my lady, you keep it. But stop into the Cross Inn before making your way to the ruins to get some more water. Tell them Oliver sent you. I'm the only Oliver in the village. Oh, and when you see a mess of rose bushes on your left, turn onto the footpath. It's a shortcut. When your foot hits cobbles, you're in the village." He patted my shoulder as I thanked him, and he continued on his way.

The footpath was no ordinary walk through the woods. It looked like a page out of a fairy tale complete with tree houses, even more rose bushes, small stone homes here and there, family grave plots, and its fair share of ancient steps. I desperately wanted to sit and write, to imagine the ghosts of these hills whispering about me, making sense out of this journey for me. Instead, I forged on until finally making it back onto the road, only stopping every so often to hold onto the guardrail, peer out into the West Yorkshire countryside, and breathe. With the last few turns of the road, I hit cobblestones. I knelt, touching them, never feeling so grateful to stand on old stones in my life. My Toms had definitely seen better days.

I saw the Cross Inn Oliver had told me about, but I was

too excited to stop. A few more turns of the hill and I was at St. Thomas' Church. I had read about the two churches in Heptonstall. The first, dating almost 1,000 years ago, had been struck by lightning. The damage had been so severe that the congregation decided to erect another church on the property instead of rebuilding. They left the old church as ruins, and it's said that over 100,000 people are buried between the old graveyard and the new one.

I entered the wrought iron gates in awe and opened Plath's *Collected Poems*[6] to "November Graveyard." "The scene stands stubborn..." it begins. In the distance were graves upon graves—some upright, some falling over, some flat tombs, others above-ground monuments and vaults. Bones, everywhere. Trees rustling in the slight breeze casted the strangest light on the field of stones, like images of little fairies dancing and playing. There were dates that I had never seen on graves before, descriptions of the way these people died—war, fever, childbirth, sleep—all forgotten, and remembered. I knew instantly what she beheld. "No dead men's cries / Flower forget-me-nots between the stones / Paving the grave ground." She saw desolation, absence, but also beauty in death. The shadows that linger long after we turn to dust. Names forever immortalize upon a hilltop of stones. Names. Names. Names. The truest words we leave behind—some that will erode with the inevitable England weather. Some that will linger with the faintest impression. I ran my fingers over the lettering, over what remained of the inscriptions, trying to seal their names in my memory. Trying to put them in a little file with Emma White.

6 Plath, Sylvia. *The Collected Poems*. New York: Harper Perennial, 1981.

I tried earnestly not to step on the moss-covered graves, but it was impossible. Far too many, much too close. I made my way to the old church ruins and entered with trepidation. It was creepy, even for a graveyard enthusiast. There were outlines of graves in there as well—people buried in the church floor, but the writing was no longer visible. I closed my eyes and saw the pews, the aisle, the ancient weddings, baptisms, and funerals—the congregants, now buried here, praying for a miracle for their parents, spouses, and children. The alter was still there with three flower bouquets tied with ribbon—a mark of today's faithful who walk among ruins.

There was a path outside the stone walls bordering the ancient graves, and I felt compelled to follow it. Immediately, I saw in the distance another cemetery—one I had seen in many pictures. This was it. I had made it. I approached the overgrown yard, only half-filled with tombstones, and felt a strange, new breeze here. I paused to welcome it before approaching the tall grass. That's when I heard a rattling. *You have got to be kidding me! I journeyed to another continent only to get attacked by rattlesnakes?* I immediately rolled down my jeans, tucking them into my Toms and turned on my cellular data to google "reptiles of West Yorkshire."

In the distance I heard a faint, "Hello? Young lady, hello? Are you looking for Sylvia?" Well, this was it. All this way and I'm not only going to die from rattlesnake bites, but also get mocked by ghosts of the dead I'm obviously disturbing. "Hello? Miss?" From behind a tree a bald old man in a sport coat and tie approached me. "Don't be afraid. I just thought you might be looking for Sylvia Plath."

"Hello, yes. I am. How did you know?" I was puzzled and shook the man's hand.

"Oh, well, there are many young women looking just like you who climb this hill to visit Sylvia." I stifled a laugh. Did we all have a look about us? White, forty-something, sweaty feminists in impractical shoes, impractical bras, and pigtail braids seeking answers to mysteries that have been pondered throughout history?

"My name is Stuart. Stuart Burns. And who might you be?" Again, I was met with kind, warm eyes.

"I'm Jen Rieger, and it has been such a long day." My own eyes welled up a bit.

"Well, you're here now. Can I show you to Sylvia?" I followed Stuart to a path just a few rows back that was a little more worn than the others. He assured me that what I had heard weren't rattlesnakes, but crickets that "seem particularly bothered for such a lovely day." Some of the stones were hard to see and looked like they hadn't been visited in years. "Yes, here we are," Stuart whispered. And there she was.

IN MEMORY
SYLVIA PLATH HUGHES
1932-1963
EVEN AMIDST FIERCE FLAMES
THE GOLDEN LOTUS CAN BE PLANTED

I sighed. I still wasn't even certain why I was there. The grave was unremarkable and a little cluttered—religious relics, dead bouquets, notes, and chipped vases lay on top.

If my grandmother had been there with me, we'd have that grave all cleaned up, just like we used to do with my relatives. We'd fold in Miracle Gro, plant new grass, and pansies would rest at the base of the stone. I knew Ted Hughes chose the quote from a Buddhist text, and the reasoning still mystified people. Looking at it at that moment, I knew. It's her. She's the fierce flame. And so am I.

"Stuart," I asked softly, "do you look after this cemetery?" Even in my very woozy, surreal mindset, I was curious about this old man.

"Oh, no. I only look after this one grave. I normally don't come here on Fridays, but oh, I don't know, something made me come here today. In any case, I made a promise to a woman twenty-five years ago to look after Sylvia, and I don't intend on breaking that promise anytime soon." I knew that her grave had been vandalized before—Plath fans scratching off the name "Hughes." Stuart showed me a picture of a woman named Jessica who had written her PhD dissertation on Plath and spent quite a bit of time in Heptonstall. "She's really very lovely, you know, and quite brilliant," he grinned, only blushing a little. I shielded my eyes to get a better look at the old man before me—his pursed smile telling me all I needed to know. It was the smile of reverence. A respect for memory and loyalty, and all that we covet. He loved Jessica, and because of her, grew to love Sylvia.

We went on to discuss my first thesis, Plath's poetry, the time she lived in the village, how his sister had known the couple and Ted's parents as well, and even about Stuart's own life. "I was born in this village," Stuart said, "and I'll die in this village. All of my relatives and ancestors are buried over yonder, dating back to, oh lord, the seventeenth century. My sister and I are the last of them. Neither one of us had any children. Just some old cats that have come and gone. We'll be buried here one day too." He smiled again, the gravity of his words not seeming to affect him. "I'll leave you to it, Jen. I have a fat cat at home waiting to be fed." I asked him if we could take a picture together and he said only if he can take one of me to give to Jessica. I gladly agreed. We snapped our pictures, shook hands, and then he stood back to kiss mine. I promised to look him up if I ever happened to scale that incline again. "If you're going to do it, do it soon, please. I'd love to see you rather than having you visit my grave." He laughed, unaffected, and slowly disappeared from the cemetery.

I sat in the overgrown grass at the foot of her grave, with my journal and pen in hand. I wrote everything—everything that entered my mind. With the sinking sun, each word became a lightening, an unburdening, a cleansing. Climbing that hill shed layers I carry with me every day. But now I had this one little journey to call my own. Would she be proud of me? Would she laugh at the ridiculousness? It's the only thing I've ever done by myself—go to a foreign country, take multiple modes of transportation into the English countryside, get lost, talk to strangers, and climb through thickets of vegetation and creepy graveyards. But I did it. Sitting at that grave, I was no longer a wife, a daughter, a mother, a teacher. I was just Jen, sitting at the feet of just Sylvia—a writer whose brilliance and talent I will never come close to, but also a woman who, sadly, did not possess my strength and resiliency. I don't know why I love her so much. I really don't. She was a genius, but so are many other writers I admire, and I won't awkwardly sit at their bones any time soon. I love her differently. She's my secret—one I take out and unwrap when I need her, wondering if her fate could have been my own. I plucked blades of grass, contemplating going back in time to help her, to be the person she telephoned that freezing cold night before she turned her kitchen into a gas chamber. But the difficult question is, would I really? There's a hidden truth—one we suppress for fear of sounding heartless. Death can be a final gift, an act of love. Hidden deep away in my desire to go back and help her is the nagging feeling that, by doing so, the poetry she left would lose its power. It's the admittance of a selfish heart, I know; but I think she knew it too. Her words empower me in the shadow of her death, whispering to me to keep going. To write. To teach. To take care of people. To climb mountains. To love.

I packed up my journal and stood memorizing the other pilgrims' artifacts left at the head of her grave. In my frantic quest to get there, I hadn't thought to bring her something. I felt around in the lint of my jeans pocket and retrieved a 2008 American penny. I squeezed it in my fist, willing some kind of magic; however, the magic was already there. My journey that day, my chance meeting with Stuart, my fingers gliding over the words on her stone, was much more of a tribute to this woman than the 85-page thesis I toiled over all those years ago. I placed the penny on her grave, and knowing I'll never see Heptonstall again, I climbed down the cobbles to the life, to the people, that awaited me.

Burn

Native Americans have burned sage for centuries as part of a spiritual ritual to cleanse a person or space.

THE SUMMER MINK

While most of my school friends spent their summers attending various camps and enrichment programs, I spent my vacation with my grandparents on "God's little acre"—a small town of freedom and familiarity. This comforted me as a child; I liked being in a place where people stopped me in the market to tell me how much I resembled my Aunt Diana, or told funny stories of my parents growing up. In Suburbia, USA, I was a nobody.

My father was a postal inspector, and the nature of his career took us all over the country—Wisconsin, Maryland, Missouri, New Jersey, Illinois, Philadelphia—but Cresson was always the constant. It's known for its scenic landscape and crystal spring water, as well as its creamy custard and front porch gossip. Years prior to my own existence, wealthy railroaders and even Andrew Carnegie vacationed in the decadent Queen Anne-style Mountain House mansions to escape the sweltering city summers. Those years are long gone, and the thriving little mountain town of railroaders and coalminers has become a bit depleted, and many struggle to get by.

While both sets of my grandparents lived in Cresson, it was an unspoken understanding that my sister and I would spend our summers with my mother's parents. I didn't question decisions like these—I knew better. There was an interesting complexity to my grandmother that the observant conversationalist could discern in a matter of minutes. She loved fresh-squeezed orange juice, clothing made with quality fabrics, porcelain dolls, and her granddaughters. As for the town itself, she possessed a love–hate relationship. An army bride at sixteen, my grandfather whisked her away from Texas and brought her to Cresson, to his family, his life. She willingly followed and gave him a daughter, but never let him forget the sacrifice she made leaving her family behind, even if they were destitute.

I suppose that's why she needed the mink coat.

Minnie Hudson[7] had a mink and wore it when there was even the slightest chill in the air—yes, even in the summer. Each Sunday in church, Grandma would stare down that mink like a gentle, skilled hunter stalking prey. She never bad-mouthed Minnie for wearing it, never openly judged her for possessing such an obvious extravagance in a blue-collar town. I watched her, the all-consuming envy gleaming in her sparkling green eyes. At the end of each service, Grandma would make her way to Minnie, feigning

7 This name has been changed.

a casual conversation. If Minnie noticed the number of times Grandma's pained, arthritic hands reached out to nonchalantly caress the coat, she never let on. I noticed though. The way her hand would linger a little longer, the way she would sigh when they parted, the way she would look at the sky as we walked home—I noticed everything. And I wished I could buy her that coat. Her crooked hand grabbed my little one. *Let's go into Altoona and get your ears pierced Babydoll, what do you say? I know your mother said no, but tiny diamonds will look so pretty.* I nodded, smiled, and kicked the rocks of the gravel alley all the way home. Grandma kicked some too.

Meyer Jonasson department store was only a few blocks away from the mall and Grandma wanted to pop in *just for a peek*. Second only to Warnaco's department store, Meyer Jonasson was the most boring place that I had ever been to in my short life. I would hide in the round clothes racks, picking pins, price tags, and lost coins off of the floor while Grandma tried on every blessed article of clothing in the store. She would stare at herself in the tri-fold mirror turning, examining, backing up, sucking in, until I would be forced to take immediate action telling her how great she looked. *For a grandma, you mean.* I reassured her that none of my friends had grandmothers as young as mine, nor did their grandmas have their ears double-pierced. That usually did the trick.

We always entered Meyer Jonasson at the shoe department, and there was a joy and pain for Grandma. So many delicious, colorful shoes awaiting perfect feet; yet, my grandma's feet were so misshapen with arthritis, she could never buy them. So we would try them on, pretend we were models—my grandma in kitten-heels that she could never sport for more than ten seconds and me in oversized three-inch heels that would surely cause instant death had I tried to actually walk. Finally, Grandma would give up. *I don't think any of these are for an old woman like me.* Practical footwear once again secured, we would head to the next department.

That's when we saw it. The mink.

Grandma casually walked over to the luxurious coat and just stood in front of it for what felt like hours. It was on sale, marked down twenty percent off.

I think you should try it on, Grandma. I sidled up softly and gently touched the coat.

It's not like the shoes, Babydoll. Coats like these are a lot of money. She looked at the price tag, trying desperately not to touch the actual fur.

Even at nine, I knew they were a lot of money, but I also knew that coat was meant for my grandma. It wouldn't hurt her hands, it wouldn't hurt her feet. It would just make her feel beautiful. And she usually didn't.

I guess it wouldn't hurt to just try it on. Grandma called the salesman over. He smiled at her choice, unlocked the precious piece, kindly helped Grandma into the mink, and guided her to the tri-fold mirrors. My breath caught as she turned with ease, her hands caressing the fur that, I thought, would only be worn by Minnie Hudson. Suddenly, she wasn't my grandma anymore. Suddenly, she was a woman staring, intently, at an alter-ego she never expected to meet. She inhaled with a sharp gasp and brought her hands to her throat.

That mink was made for you. I'll knock off an extra five percent, the handsome salesman exclaimed.

I'll take it, she whispered, without a moment's hesitation. *And I would like my initials on the lining, please. When can I pick it up?*

Unlike Minnie Hudson, Grandma rarely wore the mink coat in public. Sometimes she put it on in the house, only for me. She had to have it, had to own something of sheer indulgence; however, she was also keenly aware of what a mink coat in a declining mountain town implied.

As I walked down our staircase one cold December night, my husband stood at the coat closet unzipping the Meyer Jonasson bag that I unzipped many times as a child—just to secretly feel the silk and fur. *Here,* Ryan said. *You should wear it.* He opened the coat for me as I closed my eyes and slid my arms in. I looked down at the interior lining, and there she was, *MLG.* The white embroidered thread looked just as perfect as it did when I was nine.

When my mom gave me the coat, I thought it might just hang in my closet, as it did in hers. The irony of all of this is, the coat went to me—the bleeding heart liberal of the family who would never spend a dollar on fur.

Mom. I'm a teacher, and pretty opposed to the killing of animals for their fur. Where would I ever wear this?

Oh, stop over-thinking things, she scolded. *She'd want you to have it. Wear it to the grocery store.*

I laughed. I would not wear it to Wegman's for all of

Upper Merion to tweet about, but maybe I could wear it to a fancy restaurant in the city, or to one of my son's concerts at the Kimmel Center. If not there I could most definitely wear it to Ryan's company Christmas party with all of the Republican hunters. Hypocrite? Maybe. But I did it anyway.

This coat—my grandma's mink—I had to wear it somewhere. Deep inside of me was a little girl who remembered that look on her grandmother's face. It was a look that was about more than owning a mink like Minnie Hudson's. It was about contemplating a life that she didn't possess in that little town. It doesn't smell like her, and I didn't expect it to. But it feels like her. The silky fabric lining of the coat feels like the same silk sheets she used to put on the bed, just for me when I visited—like the same silk scarves I used to parade around the block in when my friends and I played "fashion show." It's the inside of the coat that's reminiscent of her—the soft part that's hidden from the world. The part that's meant only for me. The perfect embroidered letters *MLG* remind me of possession, and identity, and all that we value. She valued quality, but not extravagance. Feeling her around me, neither matters. I value memories.

OMENS

The first sign was my entrance. The disinfected air that smacked of refrain.

The first sign was the closet of pastels, and frills, and dolls—the tools of hypnosis passed down.

The first sign was a black capped-sleeve leotard and pink tights that bunched at the heels of perfect ballet flats.

The first sign was my grandma hiding candy that my sister wouldn't find—the way she made her salads, the way she pinched her cheeks, the way she said, *Here, Babydoll, hop on the scale for me,* then handed her an apple.

The first sign was Cinderella and all the Disney princesses with hair too big and dresses too big but smiles that said, *be me.*

The first sign was my sister's hand clutching tighter whenever we walked by the men outside the gas station, the men outside James' Drugstore, the men sitting on their front stoops. The men.

The first sign was the at the Lion's Club pool where my friends wore t-shirts over suits to hide what wasn't even there yet.

The first sign was the red stain on floral fabric and the way I balled up toilet paper so that I didn't have to tell my mom, so that I could avoid a conversation and save her from discussing sex.

The first sign was the scarlet red cheerleading uniform, wanting desperately to remain the girl they whisked into the air. Pompoms bigger than our heads, yellow mum Homecoming corsages almost just as large, and a skirt that barely covered my ass.

The first sign was *Pretty Woman* and how Julia Roberts was sexy, how Julia Roberts was funny, how Julia Roberts would never kiss on the mouth, how Julia Roberts gave blow jobs, how Julia Roberts was wanted. How Julia Roberts was saved.

The first sign was a number. A jeans size, a bra size, the pounds on the scale—numbers to haunt my sleeping and waking thoughts until food portions decreased, until their numbers got smaller, until the scale said ninety-nine and fabric would drape from my bones.

The first sign was the bartender who overserved me, whose smile and turquoise eyes entranced me, who took me for motorcycle rides, who taught me all about the first semester, who smelled of weed and Drakkar, who smirked when the words, *I'm a women's literature major*, fell from my lips.

The first sign was swearing off boys, wanting boys back, swearing boys off again, throwing their pictures into flames, all the while drinking myself stupid.

The first sign was falling in love. Falling so hard that I invented my own reality.

The first sign was leaving school to have a baby while my boyfriend finished his degree.

The first sign was the admissions officer at Villanova University who laughed at me when I asked if they had a daycare on campus for students. He smirked and said, *Why would we need that?*

The first sign was the pediatrician who told me I was paranoid when fevers spiked too high, the professor who told me to take my baby home when my sitter called out sick, the principal who hired me only after I said no to, *Will you have more babies?*

The first sign was noticing as a new teacher that most Advanced Placement classes were taught by men even though there were far more women teachers in the building.

The first sign was when my student told me a senior boy on the bus put his hand up her skirt, laughed, and told her she liked it.

One day I saw a robin trying over and over to fly through the glass of my bay window looking increasingly befuddled with each attempt. Finally a splatter of blood left its mark and she landed, a bit shaken, on the ledge of my window pane. Only then she came to. Perhaps she turned in retreat. Or perhaps she had enough. Perhaps she turned to confront an exhausting refrain, battle wounds in check.

FLAWED FEMINIST

I was a brand-new teacher, and I wanted the position. Badly. I had already sacrificed a lot to travel this new path. I sat in the conference room with two men: one, the English Department Chair I had grown to love and respect; the other, the building principal I had grown to fear. My hands, wanting to fidget, stayed calm, travelling from the starched, awkward skirt, to the glossy, imposing conference room table. "You've done a fine job as a substitute, Jen. A fine job. You've gone above and beyond." Bill Santone[8] sat at the head of the table, scanning my résumé from the glasses perched on his nose. "I just have two questions for you. One, will you ever give a student an F on a report

8 This asshole's name has been changed. He is also not to be confused with any other principal mentioned in this collection.

card, and two, are you having any more kids?" A slow grin spread across Santone's face as he took off his glasses, and I looked to my Department Chair, who was quietly analyzing his own hands.

"No to both," I replied, also smiling, trying to figure out if I pulled one over on the patriarchy with my delicious lie, or if I heard footsteps of the women's movement marching backwards in time toward the 1950s.

If the former was true, why did I hate myself?

Rachel pulled her mom-mobile into my driveway at 4 AM. We knew the traffic to Washington, DC was going to be a nightmare. It was the first full day with Donald Trump as the president, and we were heading to the Women's March for Freedom.

We had been on the phone the night before deciding what to bring in our recommended clear backpacks. Water, peanut butter sandwiches, tissues, rain ponchos, backup phone chargers, and maps—in case we got lost. I had made us both coffee. She was so cute bundled up, ready to go in her winter coat and pink scarf. She looked like the girl I had met in the English Department office almost twenty years prior, but with the eyes of a woman who had seen a lot. I set my matching protest poster in the back seat, on top of hers. On one: "Do not go gentle into that good night." On the other: "Rage, rage against the dying of the light."

We arrived at our hotel at 7 AM. The lobby was a flurry of activity. Women from all over the country had arrived with similar clear backpacks and posters, and like them, we stored our luggage with the bellman and scrutinized our map for directions. "Think there will be counter-protests?" It was something we had discussed before, and it was at the forefront of our minds. We had both read the mission statement released by the march's organizers and felt good about it; however, we also promised each other that if things got out of hand—if there was violence or flag burning—we were out. We'd ditch the posters, run back to the hotel, have a lovely dinner, and examine how far up on the "Bad Feminist List"[9] this actually put us. Minivan parked and luggage secured, we headed toward the main stage at 4th and Independence Avenue, posters hanging from our necks. We only encountered one heckler along the way—an old, bald white man who promptly told us to "get over it" as we passed him on the sidewalk.

"We have our first counter-protester!" Rachel said, loud enough for the old man to hear.

"He should probably leave the city today. He's going to a have a rough time running into people who are not 'over it,'" I yelled, just as loud.

Rachel and I approached a sea of women, with a few men speckled throughout. We were at the stage—the actual front of the stage. The pre-march program didn't start until 10:00, but I never imagined we would have rock star positions at the very front. There was a table of women cheering, high-fiving, and distributing pink "pussy hats." We laughed. Yes, they looked like cat ears, but the word choice did not go unnoticed. With Donald Trump bragging about grabbing

---

9 From Roxane Gay's *Bad Feminist*.

women by the pussy, women were reclaiming ownership of the word—a reaction of the marginalized throughout history. We both accepted the hats that came with lovely messages and e-mail addresses inside.

Dearest sister fighting the good fight:
Please know that even though I am old and cannot make it DC, I have marched for years in the name of peace and progress. I can't march anymore, but I can knit. Please wear this hat in the spirit it was made and know that I am with you today.
Love, Evelyn
Norfolk, Virginia

Rachel's message was just as sweet and sincere. We put on the hats, fixed each other's hair, and stood ready at the stage.

The posters were incredible—some empowering, some funny. Old women holding "I Can't Believe I'm Still Protesting This Shit," and young women with "Grow a Pair" and a picture of ovaries. For hours we stood, in awe, chanting, talking, meeting new people from all over the world, hearing stories of battles we never had to face. This was more than a protest; this was the pilgrimage of warning. *Beware, beware. Out of the ash I rise with my red hair. And I eat men like air.*[10]

"Think if I started a song, people would join in?"

Rachel laughed. "Why not? Give it a try."

10 Sylvia Plath's words from "Lady Lazarus" also would have made one hell of an amazing poster. Dammit.

I broke into Woody Guthrie's "This Land is Your Land," and a few voices near me quickly turned into a building crescendo from pink hats everywhere.

"Oh my God, Jen! It's working!"

One by one, invited speakers took to the stage—Gloria Steinem, Angela Davis, Cecile Richards—women we never thought we'd hear speak in person. Just a few feet away from us stood Senator Corey Booker and, oh my God, Cher too. It was surreal—a call to freedom and love that reached back in time to pluck and unveil atrocities Rachel and I never had to face. All of the sudden our everyday sexism woes that were real and hurtful in our own lives paled in comparison. We were white women of privilege. We had benefitted from the plight and the fight of others.

We marched to the White House. We chanted words of peace, we started more songs of unity, we helped each other stretch when our legs became stiff, and then when we reached the point of finally having to pee after nine hours of waiting, we marched back to our hotel, laying our posters in a memorial erected by the organizers.

The plush bed in our hotel room was inviting, but we were starving. We walked to the bar across the street and stalked a table. The place was filled with hungry marchers, and as we ordered, the waitress continued her refrain of "we're out of that." Finally, Rachel asked, "So, how about we do it this way. Could you tell us what you still have left to eat and drink?" The waitress, somewhat annoyed with her hectic night, told us they had burgers and champagne. "We'll take it."

We inhaled our burgers, toasted each other and sipped our champagne, and agreed that what we had before us was the perfect end to the perfect day.

"Jen, I can't imagine doing this march with anyone else. I really can't." Rachel looked a little teary. It wasn't the champagne; tears are not unusual for either of us.

I looked to this amazing friend—the one I loved instantly all those years ago. We had been through a lot together—the daily grind of institutional education, weddings, pregnancy, surgery, dissolved friendships, new teacher additions, new principals, sick students, injured students… dead students. "We're sisters, Rach." And it was true. She has a sister she loves; I have a sister I love. We know how to be sisters, and we're good at it. So good, in fact we've transcended blood, DNA, religious belief, and culture. We carved out a place in each other's hearts.

We returned home to find ourselves on the front page of the *Philadelphia Inquirer*, along with some other major newspapers. We were celebrities and fielding phone calls well into the night. We also returned home to social media pages that were less than complimentary. I had friends and family who vilified the marchers—vilified me. According to them (people not in attendance but had watched their chosen news source) the marchers were disrespectful, jobless rioters. More than a few of my female Facebook friends stated, "What rights are being taken away from them anyway?" I sat on my couch, staring at the glow of judgement emanating from my laptop, jaw dropped.

I guess they never had to contend with catcalls or unwanted groping, like I had. Never had to move their face back and forth and push their body away from a much stronger guy trying to kiss them, like I had. Never had men stare at their breasts instead of their eyes when having a conversation, like I had. Never had to face the stigma of a teenage pregnancy, only to have their boyfriend labeled as a "hero for staying," like I had. Never had to feel the pressure of proving themselves in teaching an Advanced Placement class, because for years those courses had typically gone to men, like I had. Never felt objectified, felt inferior. Never been called a bitch, or a slut, or a cunt. I guess they never had to carry mace just to get to class, have their head pushed down into an unzipped crotch, or call Child Line because a student was raped and pregnant. I guess they never sat in their car screaming and punching the steering wheel because their boss asked if they were going to have more babies. Like I had.

The sad part is, I know many of them have felt all of this. Maybe they believe it's the fate they were dealt way back when Eve dared to look at an apple. I refuse, so I march for them too. I'm not a perfect feminist, but I'm not a bad feminist either. I do the best I can and choose my battles wisely. I'm not the same girl who sat in that conference room while some arrogant fuck bared his teeth. I have young women, students of my past, present, and future, who are counting on me. I hold the baton. It is now my job to stand firm and see this movement through; even if it means that one day I am the one to hold a poster that says, "I Can't Believe I'm Still Protesting This Shit." Even if it means that I'm the one to sit in a rocking chair, knitting pink hats.

THE SOMETHING-ELSE

There are some things that will never just feel like a coincidence.
— A-Dack[11] Quote of the Day, May 31, 2016

The first day of school, she looked like she wanted to die. She chose the seat front and center, the perfect position for me to really appreciate her major case of RBF.[12] There were moments during my entertaining first day multimedia extravaganza when she thought about smiling. I know she did. There was a slight smirk, she'd look out the

---

11 Twitter handle and Quote of the Day handle for Anna Lendacky

12 From Urban Dictionary-
Resting Bitch Face: a person who naturally looks mean when their face is expressionless, without meaning to. *Nah, He's just got a resting bitch face. He's actually really nice.*

corner of her eye to her best friend, Dante, but then the seriousness would resume. It was, after all, AP Literature and Composition, and maybe I was particularly frightening that day with all the smiling and love.

However, it didn't take long for me to win over Anna.[13] The further we delved into the curriculum, the more she enjoyed literature, class discussion, and quietly contemplating life. She was in quite a state when she showed up for her college essay conference, bright red and full of angst. "Ms. Rieger...these people aren't going to want me. Ms. Rieger...nothing about me comes out coherently. Ms. Rieger...maybe I'll walk into traffic, or just stay here with you." How I would have loved a world in which the latter was true. It didn't take long to realize that I never wanted to let go of that RBF hot mess.

I've taught my fair share of lovely, awkward girls. I could write an entire book on each one. Chloe Steerman, one of my creative little geniuses, was constantly ripping her tights, covered in paint, and spilling coffee everywhere. Katie Burke regularly injured herself, falling in the middle of the classroom to sharpen a pencil, spilling gasoline all over her clothes trying to get to school on time. "Nobody light a match," she exclaimed while storming into my class five minutes late. Alicia-Marie Moore should have come with the label *Badass Barbie—blonde, blue-eyed, ready to embarrass herself AND kick your ass at the very same time.* Her classmates loved her, and feared her. Evana Mortezavi would stroll into my room with the aura of the goddess, Athena—strong

---

13 Not to be confused with "Everyday Sacred" Anna. Two very different girls, equally wonderful.

and lovely—and then she would share an uncomfortable, although humorous, digression during literary discussion for the entire class to hear. Cracking up at herself, she'd bellow a loud, penetrating burst of laughter. Her friend, Jon, would stare at her in disbelief. "What the hell is the *matter* with you?" All had the similar quality of being as bright as hell, loving their friends with a beautiful intensity, and not giving a shit what people thought of them. Anna doesn't know these hot mess pioneers, but she fits in quite nicely. She also doesn't know that I include myself among them. Merge together their awkwardness, and you have the high school version of Jen Rieger. I too could career down a flight of stairs with the grace of Melissa McCarthy. I too could acquire a bee sting on my ass while cheering at a homecoming game. I have a special bond with these girls. I sympathize with them and at the same time applaud their ability to generate chaos and put smiles on faces whenever they walk, or fall, into a room.

As the year progressed, my sweet friendship with Anna developed. She became my little sidekick—my Quote of the Day girl, sometimes reflecting her humorous nature, sometimes her sentimental heart. She and Dante would stay after school chatting with me about high school life and college decisions, and she and her friend, Alex, would hang out in my room when they had study hall and I had a free period. Sometimes we'd work on the next paper due, sometimes we'd stuff our faces with breakfast junk foods. She embraced our school's Challenge Day program, becoming one of my facilitators, and we both vehemently scrutinized and abhorred the newest trend in thick, stenciled eyebrows. She also shared with me her growing anxieties about moving on. Anna hated change—feared it. Whether it was rearranging the desks in my room, darkening my hair, or trading in my Jeep Wrangler for a new car, she didn't want any of it. I guess that's why when she overheard a conversation with one of my colleagues about my impending sabbatical, she looked like she had been punched in the gut. "What do you mean you won't be here next year? How is that even possible?" I reminded her that she won't be here either. She will be in college, learning, making new friends, and loving life. "But you're supposed to stay right here. Where I can find you."

She did graduate, begrudgingly. She did move onto college, begrudgingly. Anna is wise, very wise. She spent her senior year growing up, analyzing relationships, perfecting the fine art of holding on and trying to perfect letting go. Growing up means change, and that is some very real and scary shit.

When I picked her up at her St. Joe's University dorm one warm September night, she knew the moment of truth had arrived. It was just the two of us—no Dante or Alex to hide behind when I pelted her with questions. She wasn't embracing school. She was going home on the weekends, travelling to Penn State to visit her high school friends, mourning a beautiful past she was forced to relinquish. We sat at the bar in Chili's on City Line Avenue, inhaling bottomless chips and salsa.

"Riegs... I can pass for twenty-one. A margarita would be great with these chips."

I laughed, "Child, did you just meet me? Plus, you can

barely pass for fifteen, and you know it."

She sipped her water, I sipped my Diet Coke, and we discussed classes, roommates, and my new schedule. "Okay, spill it," I finally said. "Imagine it's period 2 study hall. Time to unload." Similar to my own, her brown eyes take on a shade of green when they fill with tears. It happens to her quite often when she's sad, but also when she encounters beautiful poetry, beautiful moments, and beautiful people. We sat at that bar for hours discussing everything, right down to the meaning of life. Growing up is hard. Really hard. I know she had hoped that going to school in Philadelphia would mean not *completely* leaving home. But it did. Home isn't necessarily a place—and it isn't necessarily people. It's a feeling that evolves and breaks us into a renewed sense of self. She missed home. She needed to reclaim it. But she also needed to understand that it takes time.

When I drove her back to her dorm, she said she wouldn't cry anymore. "I know, Riegs. I won't. For now. And I'll try to accept your ugly new car, even though you're supposed to be driving a cool Jeep Wrangler." With a heavy eyeroll, I nodded, understanding her need for a nostalgic constant. As she trekked across the pavement to her building, I saw my eighteen-year-old self in the shadow moving across the ground. And I willed that girl to be strong. I willed her to make me proud.

So she did.

On January 20th, as I packed for my journey to the Women's March for Freedom in Washington, DC, I sent a text to Anna. She spent winter break having the time of her life with her high school friends, and while I was thrilled for her, I was also worried about her. "How was your week back? Please tell me you're going out and doing something fun tonight." She sent back a video of t-shirts and posters with written messages of peace and empowerment. She was going to the march. "I'm doing something much more fun than going out." With laughter and chatter of all her new friends in the background of the video, indeed she was. And it wasn't just this. She made the leap we all have to make during difficult transitions—she made a decision to be the heroine of her own life.

I'm not a mom to this girl. I'm not a friend. I'm not a teacher anymore either. I'm a something-else; she's a something-else. I can't define it, but then again, the majority of the most beautiful, important concepts in life can't be defined. Quality, love, peace, God—we use these words on a daily basis, not really understanding their encompassing magic when our lives appear to revolve around them. What I do know is that extra room in my house—the one that was supposed to be a nursey—doesn't feel so haunting anymore. I know whatever I have with this child has to do with energy, connection, and family. I feel her pain, even when she thinks she hides it. I feel her joy, even when she thinks she's containing it. It's like we all have these little soulmates roaming around the world, and it's our job to find them and recognize their beauty and purpose in our lives. Maybe it sounds overly new-agey, but Anna sees it too. For Christmas she bought me a little pin—a grape jelly jar. She has the other one that came with it—a peanut butter jar. And maybe that's what we are, since I'm not the mom, the friend, or the teacher. Maybe I'm the jelly. I'll take it.

THE GREAT EQUALIZER

We embrace myth, not just as a representation of culture and history, but as means of universal communication. Even when there is a language barrier, myth connects us. We no longer believe in monsters like Polyphemus or Scylla and Charybdis, but we go back to these tales to advocate for heroes, to remember valuable lessons: seek good, conquer evil, keep pride in check, find meaning. Myth becomes personal—we hold it to collected unconsciousness and use it to make sense of reality in times of need. Maybe that's why we're surrounded by saints on this little island of Ortigia. They lived. They were here, once upon a time. Were they exaggerated? Did they really perform miracles? Does it matter? The plight of St. Lucia, the relics of St. Thérèse, and the alter of St. Peter offer solace and hope—something that will be around long after we're all gone.

As I walked through the Capuchin catacombs in Palermo, Sicily, I thought of this, that is, those myths we cling to in times of need. Almost 500 years ago, when the catacombs were created, Brother Silvestro Da Cubbio's body was prepared—drained of blood, organs removed, flesh dried out, and he was put into a wall niche on display, and celebrated on Giorno dei Morti, or the Day of the Dead. Upon their deaths, other monks joined him, then honorary members of Palermo's society—military members, writers, artists, government leaders—thousands of them. Their remains line the walls, eroding away, their bones falling into each other with the progression of time, their jaws dropping. Some look in pain and horror, others as if they are laughing at the morbid spectacle they left behind. They once walked this earth just as we all do, working, playing, making love, making mistakes, looking for comfort and peace. They must have thought, at least at some point, that they had all the time in the world. But the bones, in various states of aged disrepair and decay, the dates pinned onto the rags that once were clothes, remind us that we will all be there. Joseph Addison asserts this in his essay "Meditations on Westminster Abbey"—it's our greatest commonality. Rich, poor, intelligent, simple, the dust of kings will mingle with the dust of paupers. We will one day be recognized in the faint phenotype that mark future faces—only to be recognized in the brilliance of stardust.

I found myself in the "bambino" hall of the ancient crypt, studying the miniature skeletal faces. Some of the babies were curled up in cradles, others positioned on rocking chairs holding a sibling's hand. Once I got past the sheer horror of what I was actually seeing, my mind was consumed with what their parents must have felt upon visiting them here for the first time. How their mothers must have sobbed and prayed to the saints for the souls of their babies. How, even in their state of decomposition, they must have felt compelled to take them from the walls to cradle and hold, to love the remaining bones that were once animated with flesh and sweetness.

I made my way to the temperature-controlled glass casket that held Rosalio Lombardo—"Sleeping Beauty." She died of pneumonia at the age of two and her father, so overwhelmed with grief, hired an embalmer to preserve her. Unlike the other bambinos of the crypt, her face, like a plastic little doll, dons a look of perpetual sleep. Her blue eyes opened just a slit, her cheeks blushed red, she actually looks like she still suffers from the fever that took her back in 1920. There is a local legend that she opens and closes her eyes each day, but scientists maintain that it is only an optical illusion—the angle of the light from the nearby window tricking visitors into the hope of another saintly miracle.

I'm not sure how long I stood there. The nearby noise of a youth soccer game and a child's song faintly echoed in the hall. From the beginning of this writers' retreat, I had been excited to be a part of the creepy, morbid tourist attraction. After all, I'm the girl who thoroughly enjoys the occasional stroll around ancient cemeteries, reading unique epitaphs on tombstones, honoring those who came before us. I'm the one who climbed a mountain to sit at the feet of my favorite dead poet. But this. This was something entirely different. Finally, I looked down the hallway of the long-tunneled catacomb, thousands of bodies lining the walls, and I was alone. Completely alone. I wasn't scared. Just very still and very small. "Your mother loved you very much," I whispered to the little doll. I don't cry at the cemeteries I visit, I didn't cry at the grave of Sylvia Plath, I don't cry when I visit the graves of my loved ones, but I cried for this little girl's mother. I've been to enough student funerals and have seen the look on enough mothers' faces—the look that doesn't even have a word in the English language to describe that kind of grief and emptiness. It is a look that says, "I may roam this earth for years to come, but I'm not really here. I am simply a shell of a person—the moribund. The walking dead." Rosalio's mother isn't mentioned in any of the literature about this sleeping child—only the grief of her father, in desperate need to preserve this baby.

I backed away from the glass casket; the blue from the slits of her eyes remained. Head down, I walked the tunneled halls of the dead wanting only sunshine, wanting only escape. As I left the cold, dry crypt, I passed the souvenir shop and saw her—the Virgin Mary on a half-euro postcard among the pictures of the catacomb's dead. With a subtle, peaceful grin, she told me not to cry. Not to worry. Not to dwell on the looks of skeletal horror that had just surrounded me. She's smiling in radiance at all my doubt and skepticism of the faithful—those who pray to her for guidance, those who would buy that postcard. Saint Mary, the ultimate symbol of maternal pain, smiling, because peace will come. We know this through the stories we pass down, the stories we seek out in times of need. We will live, we will die, and we hope to leave some goodness with those who remain so they can provide comfort. So they, like the saints, can radiate the light found in the stars.

BURNING SAGE

I lie on the table waiting, too tired to sit, and the doctor is taking forever. She always does. I've known her for over twenty years, and I'm convinced she is the one in the practice hypochondriacs request. She holds our hands, lets us cry, and listens. I don't live in this town anymore, but I drive the hour to see her. She gets me.

She enters the room and we exchange greetings as she holds my shoulder to help me sit up.

"The lump is there again," I say.

She feels my neck, checks my throat, looks in my ears, my nose. "Say 'Ahh.' Okay, now swallow for me." I do as she presses. Her hands move to my glands. "How's your son?"

She always asks about Evan, and I'm never quite sure what to say.

Today, however, I want to gut myself open and tell her everything. That time slipped away so much more violently than the clichéd grains of sand on a television hourglass, and I didn't even realize it. I want to explain how and why I royally fucked it all up, letting the minutia of my career eat away precious hours when Evan needed a mom, not a sister. How I was so intent on proving everyone wrong and dispelling the teen-mom stigma I had to lug on my back like a weighted training camp backpack while Ryan was deemed a hero. How when my mother snapped with, "You think you're going to finish school with a baby?" I had to stand on a mountain and yell *HOLD MY BEER* for all of the world to hear and shake the graves of my grandmothers. How everything comes at a price, and there's no such thing as women having it all. How "teaching is such a great career for moms" is the biggest myth that was ever invented because you love them like your own. You lie awake at night worrying, not just about your own child asleep down the hall, but *thousands*, all with their own unique demons. How these past few years since Evan left for college, I've inadvertently been piecing together this mosaic of other people's children in an attempt for...what? Some kind of final exam redo? Any artist will tell you that the reality of the mosaic is that they are still broken. It becomes an elaborate attempt for beauty and order out of fractured chaos. Those students leave. And if they do return, it's not the same. I want to scream into the sterile walls of that tiny exam room and tell her everything became a sacrifice—a tradeoff. All of this I learned far too late. And some choices can't be undone.

But I don't say any of this.

"He had another rough semester. I didn't see him much this year. I think he's sad a lot." I stare at my hands wondering again when they started looking exactly like my mother's.

"Uh huh." She adjusts her stethoscope in her ears and places the chest piece over my heart, her other hand on my back. "Breathe for me." I do, inhaling and exhaling deeply. "Are you still doing yoga?"

I avert my eyes. "No. Not for a while now."

"I see. Let me just listen to your heart a bit. See if it will tell me anything more than these short responses you're giving me." She winks. "Tell me about your seniors this year."

I smile. "They were amazing. My favorite class ever. I think. Maybe it's too soon to tell." Her grin is a giveaway. She's heard this from me before.

"Who were you closest to?" She sits on the rolling stool, still listening, but looking through my chart.

"Three boys. The two are twin brothers, the other is their best friend. They're just...lovely human beings." I look to the ceiling as she stands up.

"Let me feel that lump again." She places her fingertips on my throat, the other hand on the back of my head. She then cups my face with her hands, something she does often. "Jen. It's June. You've done this to yourself before. The knot you're feeling will go away in a few weeks. You know it's simply a globus brought on by the stress you've experienced. You know that."

My eyes well. "It's different this time. They're different.

And they're gone."

"I know. And they get to take your love with them. You gave that to them. But now you have to recharge. Okay? You keeping up with your anxiety management?"

I nod.

"Good girl. Get yourself to the beach, please, and away from that town. Oh, and back to yoga! You know how much you love it." She hands me a business card. "Here's the number of an ENT specialist if you want to make an appointment, but I would give it a few weeks. Okay?" She hugs me. "You're a love."

It's the exact phrase I use with my kids.

I lie on the table, waiting. With the exception of the bikini bottom, I'm naked, but warm under the blanket. Walking into the spa was a last minute decision, and I'm covered in sunblock, mixed with a bit of sand. The ocean is a few blocks away, but the sound system reverberates a harmony of artificial waves breaking under a soft acoustic guitar. My massage therapist is on the other side of the door. I hear him shuffling through the questionnaire I filled out. No medical problems to report. Areas of discomfort: Neck and upper back.

He walks in and places his hand on my covered foot. "Comfortable?"

"Yes. Thank you," I lie. I haven't been comfortable for some time. I'm face up, and he rubs lemongrass oil into his hands and hovers them over my face before lowering them to my forehead, then to my temple.

"Breathe in for me. A big inhale." I comply, breathing in the fresh aroma. "Now exhale slowly. Let go of whatever is on your mind. Release it to the ocean." I stifle a laugh, trying to dismiss every New Age platitude I conjure. He begins to work on my shoulders, sensing the knots I've been carrying for months. His hands move to my neck and he stops, asking me to swallow. He presses gently on my throat.

"There's a sadness here. It's locked in your throat."

I want to jump off the table. I want to tell him he's a crazy old hippie who doesn't have a clue what he's talking about. I want to tell him I'm fine.

Instead, I cry.

It's the same cry that consumed me graduation night when I sat in my Jeep at the Villanova Pavilion, after everyone had left, crying for children who aren't mine. Children with families of their own. Children who will return home from college to their own mothers who will cook them favorite dinners, wash their clothes, and listen about their new lives. Other people's children.

I don't tell the therapist any of this. He doesn't expect me to. He grabs a cool, damp towel that smells of lavender and wipes the tears from my face and ears. "Take three deep breaths," he whispers. I calm myself down, and he continues the session, working through the kinks and knots that grip me, occasionally wiping a stray tear that slips through.

After the session is over, he meets me in the hallway with a glass of water and a paper bag. I'm feeling better, but the lump is still there, reminding me of its presence with each large gulp. "Hydrate throughout the day and avoid alcohol. It's poison." I want to roll my eyes, but he hands me the paper bag. I look inside and see a plastic bag with three giant joints—or what look like three giant joints. I begin to laugh. I must be a serious fucking mess if this guy is just handing me his weed. "It's not marijuana," he laughs. "It's sage. Burn it. Vanquish your ghosts. Let them go."

I sit at the table, smiling at the faces of the boys I said goodbye to six months ago. We created our own field trip, meeting at the train station in Philadelphia and making our way to the Rosenbach Museum to stare at old books and immerse ourselves in favorite authors. Brian and Alex are English majors, Andrew is a business major. Brian is genius and probably the smartest and most diligent English student I've ever taught. The twins are well aware of this and also realize that our bookish expedition is really for the two of us. Both would much rather catch an Uber and head to the Philadelphia Sports Museum, but they're also gracious souls and willing to indulge in a day of Brian ooohing and ahhh-ing over ancient books.

"Can I hear some of your favorite authors?" the tour guide asks. Our group offers up names—Melville, Plath, Joyce, Hemingway, Morrison. She gets to Andrew. "I'm not sure if you've heard of him. Famous author by the name of Dr. Seuss." I grin at my little class clown while his twin brother and friend shake their heads. They're used to his sarcastic comebacks. The tour guide smirks and rolls her eyes; she's not impressed.

I take them for pizza afterwards at Serafina's, an Italian restaurant in Rittenhouse Square. White linen tablecloths, white cloth napkins folded into flowers, Italian opera permeating the oregano-imbued air. We feel fancy.

"Let's order calamari and make Brian try it." The twins agree that this is a brilliant idea, and Brian looks like he wants to die.

"I mean, I'll do it. It might not be pretty," Brian shrugs. We laugh.

We discuss books and memories, new professors and college parties. Alex excitedly recounts some antics from the fall. "We totally lost Brian. He got wasted and ended up passed out under a tree for hours. We had to call his brother to help us find him and everything." Brian's face turns a nice shade of crimson. I had already heard the story but settle into my natural teacher-lecture-mode.

"Guys. Binge drinking, really? Brian, you're smarter than these two knuckleheads! Don't be a dumbass. And you two—Brian usually takes care of everyone. Can you please watch out for him when he decides to turn into a disaster? And let me remind all three of you—you're nineteen! You have the rest of your lives to act like fools." I give my best stern mom-look, even though I secretly love this familiar banter of stories they would not have shared with me a year ago.

Alex rolls his eyes. Out of the three, he's the one I'm closest to. He's had a rough few months leaving high school behind and finding his footing, but he's making it. He's the one who came to me with everything, from death and love to project woes and inside jokes. He made that blue chair his home.

"Oh, calm down, Jen. You know we've got this." Alex winks, and Brian and Andrew stare at him, wondering if he has lost his mind.

"Jen?" I question. "You're out of my classroom for six months and moving onto Jen?" Andrew scoffs. Brian looks horrified.

"The disrespect, Alex! Don't piss off the woman buying us lunch." Brian always has my back, no matter the situation. I'm also fairly certain when he's fifty years old, he will still be calling me Ms. Rieger.

"Ehh. I'm trying it out. Seeing how it feels. After all, I'm going to teach with her one day." Alex pops another calamari in his mouth.

His brother shakes his head. "Yeah. In your dreams. Like they'd hire *you*."

"Fuck you, Drew." Alex throws a piece of calamari at him, and they all laugh. It's the laughter of youth, the sound that keeps me going when years are rough— when bureaucracy constrains my professional autonomy in thick red tape or when the proverbial bell jar lingers ever so slightly above my head. It's the sound of magic.

My mind is transported back to one year ago and, as I look at these faces, the word *Quality* churns over and over. Every year my incoming seniors read Robert Pirsig's philosophical novel, *Zen and the Art of Motorcycle Maintenance*, and his capitalized variation of Quality haunts the air of my cinderblock classroom. *Quality* is the quest. It's what the driven soul strives for, and what lingers in the corners of minds in the face of mediocrity. Quality is the Goodness—the God, the top of the mountain we aim for.

These faces. These smiles. Today, they're the balm. And it feels like home.

I lie on the blanket in the sand. It's January, but unseasonably mild. I had walked the beach for miles that morning, watching the fierce waves try to meet me with each ebb of the ocean. A recent storm turned up some pieces of sea glass and a broken sand dollar, and I remove my gloves to brush off the sand and pocket my winter treasures.

The two thick blankets I brought invite me. I huddle under the one while unpacking my books, journal, and thermos of chai tea. The sun is bright, and the sky is much bluer than I've seen in quite a while. I reach my arm deep down into the bottom of the beach bag that hasn't seen the outdoors since August. I scavenge around until I feel it—the brown bag and lighter I had packed away last July. I carefully unfold the crinkled paper, extracting the three rolls of dried sage. They've remained in the undisturbed plastic for six months—I wasn't even sure I was ever going to open it.

They're still my kids. They always will be, no matter how old they get. For whatever reason—fate, chance, the magic of class scheduling software—our lives entwined like garden vines. We try our best, getting together twice a year, but it's not the same.[14] I get fragments of their lives through impromptu texts—baseball, frat parties, college debt, essay help, love interests, heartbreaks, political rants, and existential crises. The blue chair in my classroom has transformed itself into three digital glowing text threads of growing up, moving on, and letting go.

I light all three rolls, fan them with my book to get the embers going, and stick them in the sand. As the January light becomes soft and hazy, each roll burns into the damp divots I created for them. The smoke transforms into shadowy clouds, billowing the salt air until, ultimately, they dissipate to another time and place. I watch the dried leaves extinguish themselves, until finally, finally, the high tide comes for all that remains, and the knot loosens, just a bit.

---

14 It's not the same; however, Brian became my student teacher and Alex was just hired to teach tenth grade English across the hall from me. The universe is funny that way.

THERE IS A ROAD, NO SIMPLE HIGHWAY

I stand in the solitude of the waterfall. It's cold and rainy, the exact kind of weather that makes me want to crawl back under a weight of heavy blankets. But today, there's something about the Oregon air. My lungs feel like they're inhaling a thousand years of Zephyr's sweetness, come just a bit early. Did I ever taste and smell air this delicious? At home, rain smells of pavement. My new hiking boots are a mess—a mark of the terrain I had covered that morning. It wasn't an easy hike to get here—centuries-old roots splitting the ground along each path, heavy winter branches catching my coat. I spotted four or five other hikers braving the damp chill of the falls that morning, so I followed their lead through the muddy trails.

I'm at the midpoint of my Pacific coast journey. I had run Seattle's frigid waterfront, sipped wine at the top of the Needle, strolled the streets of Bainbridge Island, and investigated cozy bookstores and coffee houses. I braved the pouring rain of Portland, finding refuge in its unique wine bars and its gigantic literary-nerd mecca of Powell's Books. It's my solo-journey—a new adventure. I had promised myself after walking down the cobblestones of Heptonstall that my ongoing quest to eradicate fear would not stop at the bones of Sylvia Plath. I had spent over forty years as someone's daughter, over two decades as someone's wife. Little by little I decided to shake trepidation from the attic of my mind and sweep away the cobwebs of my mother's greatest fears. *No, you can't do that by yourself. No, you can't drive in the city. You must be home by 10:30. No, you can't go to the concert.* And then, after I met Ryan... *Please tell me Ryan is going with you. Everywhere.* I scared her. I've always scared her. But I get it.

The other hikers seemed to have vanished. I turn to see the seclusion of green woods, moss-covered trees so bright they almost look painted, only the sound of water echoing. I'm cold and should probably leave, but I can't seem to depart from this exquisite moment. I take a few steps closer to the water, zipping my phone in a plastic baggie I remembered to pack for such an occasion. I bend to the agitated pool before me, my hand touching the icy water. I bring it to my lips.

I was in search of an initiation, and a departure from the ordinary, so I took a "professional compensated leave." When I ran the idea past my principal, Jonathan, he cocked his eyebrow, like he's known to do, smiled and said, "Of course you should do this. But we both know it's going to be hard on you." My life sometimes feels like the movie *Groundhog's Day*. Each year, I greet the same age group of students; each year I discuss the same twelfth grade requirements; each year I try to vary the literature but inevitably teach the similar lessons grounded in different plots, I relay the same stories, tell the same jokes; each year I don my cap and gown and watch them walk across the stage at graduation. I had already accomplished a great deal in the past year—studied at the University of Oxford, participated in an international writers' workshop in Sicily, had my writing published. I took my life off a shelf, dusted it off, stared at it for a bit, and reevaluated. At home, I'm a presence—the master of ceremonies to the daily monotonous show for high school seniors. Here, I'm just an iPhone pindrop in an immense, ancient forest. In all its majesty, my thoughts still turned to home. My kids would be in ninth period reading Frost's "Fire and Ice" with their substitute. They'd start Blake's "The Tyger" at the end of class if the discussion died out too soon. I wondered if she reminded them to bring their poetry books. I wondered if Amy had a light-hearted Quote of the Day on the board, if Lucy heard from any other schools, if Brian was okay, if Semaj finished the essay he promised, if Rachel was eating lunch by herself.

I knew I couldn't torture myself—knew I couldn't stare at the clock like I used to do when Evan first went to daycare. Wondering. Wondering. *What are they doing now?*

Now I stare at a waterfall instead of students' faces.

"Hey there! You're awfully close to that fall. Don't slip. I'm not the best in emergencies, and it looks like we're the only two out here."

I turn to find a small woman carrying a backpack relatively the same size as her. She's wearing hiking boots that look like mine and a waterproof jacket that looks like mine. As she approaches, I grab her hand, helping her to a nearby rock.

"Have you been out here long?" She projects her small voice in an effort to outdo the loudness of the crashing water and shields her face from the mist.

"Not long. Maybe about twenty minutes." It occurs to me that twenty minutes is actually a long time to stare at rushing water.

"It's really so gorgeous. I've been here a few times, but never this close. I can feel the negative ions in my lungs, can't you?" She steps back, at a safer distance, and I follow her. She's super cute. Her eyes are a bright green, and I wonder if the surrounding lichen intensify the hue. There's a dreamy lilt to her voice reminding me of a favorite waitress at one of our local restaurants in Philadelphia who is just as cute, and also perpetually high. She closes her eyes, inhaling and exhaling, in a sort of rhythmic meditation.

I make my way back onto the muddy path and think of a word I've been turning over again and again in my mind. *Shul*—a Hebrew word. Traditionally it means school, or temple—a place of learning. It also implies the sacred impression of something that was once there. A footprint on a path. The bones of an abandoned house that was once filled with love. The mark that remains. "Would you mind taking a picture for me? I haven't done a great job getting myself in these landscapes." I extract my phone from its plastic bag and she gladly takes it, carefully snapping different shots, different angles.

"There's a bridge with benches just a short ways away. I was headed there to take this pack off and rest for a bit if you want to join me. Oh, I'm Colleen, by the way. You are?" I tell her my name and accept her offer, hoping it doesn't take me too far off my trail.

We walk another path, and as we move further from the waterfall, the air warms, just a bit. It doesn't take any time to find the bridge and the benches. I still see the trail that leads straight back to my rental car. I'm not lost.

Colleen takes off her pack with an audible groan, moves her shoulders in circles, and touches her toes. "I feel like I could jump straight to the top of that fall!" We laugh. She opens the side pocket of her backpack and removes a bottle, that has the exact faux-wood finish as mine. "Do you like rose petal tea? I have an extra little cup in here too." I had never tried rose petal tea before, but as she opens the bottle, I smell the roses blending with the forest's lush scent. It's heaven, and I suddenly realize how thirsty I am.

She pours some for me into a little tin mug she retrieved. "To magical encounters," she says. We toast and sip the warm liquid. I could hear my mother's voice reverberating in my head. *What if she's poisoning you? What if it's a ploy to harvest your organs?* I look at this tiny being, chirping away about her own adventure through the forests of the Pacific Northwest, and I decide to block my mother's voice from my mind.

Colleen's thirty-eight and originally from Colorado. She endured a messy family life, and woke up one day, bought a van, and decided to travel the country. "I've been socking away money for years, and now, this is what I do."

We talk for an hour. She listens to my life of teaching, writing, and separation issues, and I listen to her life of van troubles, pathetic relationships, even more pathetic sex, and finding peace. Her eyes tell of the pain she veils. I've encountered those kinds of eyes before—sometimes during parent conferences, sometimes from the desks in my classroom, sometimes from Evan's sweet face. They're the kind of eyes that make me cry.

When we part ways, we shake hands, and she grips a little tighter. "You are a lovely human being," she says, putting both hands over mine. "I can feel your soul."

I find my footpath toward my rental car and the sun appears, just a bit, through the branches of the sequoias surrounding me. I stop in the silence, look up into the warmth, and hold onto a thick trunk nearby. It's been here for centuries. It's withstood a lot. It will continue to withstand.

So will I.

Extracting my journal from my pack, I sit in the hollowed crotch of the tree, not caring about the dirt or the moss. I sit at the base, breathing in the world, and I write of everything that's brought me to this point and everything that will bring me back home. I write of grandmothers and childhood, stigma and gumption, love and ghosts, God and Quality. I write of my kids—all of them merging into their own separate archetypes yet uniquely imprinted in my mind as if those thousands were meant to be mine. I write of this unexpected career that was supposed to be the meantime—the meantime that led me to my path and gave me purpose. Maybe I'm still that young girl trying to figure out over twenty years of faces, moments, days, classes. I spend my life snapping hundreds of pictures to remind myself that they're real—that they were actually in my grasp for a short time. And that Evan was the one who brought me to them all. When I learned the content, designed the lessons, wrote my thesis, and attended countless workshops on standardized tests, nobody explained how to handle the sorrow that comes with this beautiful, frightening job—the letdowns, the bureaucracy, the losses, the goodbyes.

But they also didn't tell me about the joy.

Maybe the *meantime* has always been *my time*. Maybe this was the trajectory predestined in the stars, if you believe in that sort of thing. Maybe I won't be recognized for the hundreds of pages I've composed. It's okay. Maybe my kids are my poem—some stanzas free verse, some structured, some with short line breaks, and some with enjambment that continues well past graduation day. All contributing to the verse of my life. All making my time here worth it.

ACKNOWLEDGMENTS

Earlier versions of the following essays have been published in the following magazines and journals:

"The Meantime"- *Role Reboot Magazine*
"The Summer Mink"- *The Manifest-Station*
"Elegy"- Her Verse (Personal blog)
"Becoming Jen"- *BUST Magazine*
"The Fix"- *Philadelphia Stories*
"Union Cemetery"- *The Wisconsin Review*
"Curse, Bless Me"- *Philadelphia Stories*
"You Mean Ted Hughes' Wife?"- *Chautauqua Literary Journal*

All photography and cover art by Khanh Nguyen.
Thank you…
… to my writing "muses"—Carla Spataro, Liz Abrams-Morley, Marshall Warfield, and Anne Kaier. They have inspired me with their love of teaching, craft, and beauty.
… to my MFA sisters, Rae Pagliarulo, Kara Cochran, Kat Hayes, Maria Ceferatti, and Mary-Kate Kaminski, who are some of the loveliest and most brilliant people I have had the pleasure of working with and knowing.
… to my Upper Merion friends for helping me on this journey, cheering me on since I was a twenty-four-year-old, and being awesome "other-parents" to Evan. Additionally, my everlasting appreciation to my best friends and fellow teachers, Jeff Bugenhagen, Rachel Darnell, and Jason

Darnell, for always remaining true to our shared vision of supporting and believing in the children we love—for being my family.

… to my sister, Kim Reichard, for holding my hand at every coastline, convincing me that I had the biggest heart; to my dad, Ken Weaver, for instilling in me fearlessness and the constant reminder to remain true to myself; to my mom, Sandy Weaver, for telling me from a very young age that I was smart, I was creative, and I was born to be a writer.

… to my graduates, Alex Del Giudice, Andrew Del Giudice, Brian Loane, and Anna Lendacky, for allowing me to pick their magnificent young minds and utilize their extraordinary talents. There are some kids that I just don't get in the classroom long enough but thank goodness they've remained my little friends well past graduation day.

… to all of my kids—past, present, and future— those who are mentioned in these pages, and those who are not, my eternal gratitude for shaping my life and giving me purpose.

… and to Ryan and Evan, the loves of my life, for absolutely everything.

JENNIER L. RIEGER

Jennifer Rieger is a public educator and college professor in the Philadelphia area. An advocate for her students and graduates, she dedicates her time to empowering others through reading, writing, and acts of love. Jen has been honored with the Franklin Institute 2020 Excellence in Teaching Award, the 2021 Philadelphia Phillies All-Star Teaching Award, and was a semi-finalist for the Pennsylvania Department of Education Teacher of the Year. Along with a nomination for the 2020 Pushcart Prize for Literature, she's also been published in *Chautauqua Literary Journal, Wisconsin Review, BUST Magazine,* and *Philadelphia Stories 15th Anniversary Anthology,* among others. Jen holds an MA in English Literature, an MFA in Creative Writing, and spends her free time bragging about her son, students, and thousands of graduates.